Best Wishes for a Happy Christmas. <u>1990</u>

Fred Seetley

SHAUN HILL'S
GIDLEIGH PARK
Cookery Book

SHAUN HILL'S
GIDLEIGH PARK
Cookery Book

Foreword by Ted Hughes

CENTURY

London Sydney Auckland Johannesburg

To Anja

First published in 1990 by Century Editions,
an imprint of The Random Century Group Ltd,
20 Vauxhall Bridge Road, London SW1V 2SA

Random Century (Australia) Pty Ltd,
20 Alfred Street, Milsons Point, Sydney,
New South Wales 2061, Australia

Random Century New Zealand Ltd, PO Box 40-086,
Glenfield, Auckland 10, New Zealand

Random Century South Africa (Pty) Ltd,
PO Box 337, Bergvlei, 2012 South Africa

British Library Cataloguing in Publication Data
Hill, Shaun *1947–*
Shaun Hill's Gidleigh Park cookery book.
I. Title
1. Food – Recipes
641.5
ISBN 0-7126-3603-X

Editor Susan Fleming
Design Bob Vickers
Illustrations by Jeremy Ford

Typeset by Vision Typesetting, Manchester
Colour origination by Colorlito, Milan
Printed and bound in Spain by Graficas Estella, sa

CONTENTS

FOREWORD

The great poet John Keats's most famous words, perhaps, were: 'O for a life of sensations rather than thoughts!' – when he peppered his tongue to intensify the engulfing splendour of a claret. His passion for fine foods produced some of the most excited moments in his poems. During the spring of 1818, when he was staying at Teignmouth – the mouth of the River Teign – on the south Devon coast, his gastronomic priorities were alert, and he wrote some doggerel to his friend Haydon, the painter:

> Here all the summer could I stay,
>> For there's a Bishop's Teign,
>> And King's Teign,
> And Coomb at the clear Teign's head;
>> Where, close by the stream,
>> You may have your cream
> All spread upon barley bread.
>
>> There's Arch Brook,
>> And there's Larch Brook,
> Both turning many a mill;
>> And cooling the drouth
>> Of the salmon's mouth,
> And fattening his silver gill.

Then he let the yolk-yellow flowering furze bushes distract him as they clawed at a maiden's gown, and the maidens making merry after nightfall in Newton Abbot Market Street, and then again by primroses (which probably reminded him of the pale, mingled yellows of the Devon clotted cream), and the violets silvered in a wet, April light on the thousand-year-old hedgebank under the hollow tree with its wild bees (he was probably remembering the connoisseur's combination of clotted cream and honey). Did he walk all the way upriver (he was a great walker) to Teigncombe?

If he did it again now, he would meet some surprises. The first surprise, maybe, would be to see how little has changed in the secret valley of the Teign. No mills working, fewer cottages and maybe fewer people, but the same river pools, under their vaulted ceilings of oak boughs, under the same hanging woods and steep fields with their sheep, under the same roundy Devon hilltops that bulge above the woods like the tonsured domes of fat monks, the same granite monastery farms tucked into their folds. He could see the same shoals of sea-trout (even more delicately flavoured than the salmon) aligned like fleets at anchor under the greeny-golden flow of the Teign, and maybe, in a lucky sun-shaft, the same salmon, moving their gills. And up above him, here and there, a buzzard turning in a therm, mewing and yelping to its mate somewhere, or maybe just for sheer joy, and maybe teased by a raven – all the same. He might be surprised, too, to hear that in few other places in England could he now enjoy just that mix of pleasures.

But the big surprise is to come – further upstream. He's already thinking about his primrose clotted cream and barley bread – at Teigncombe.

So he pushes past Dunsford, up through a narrowing gorge, the pools twistier and noisier, the woods hanging out of the sky, and comes on through the hollow parkland clearing below Chagford, and glimpses the hilltops looking higher, unfarmed, rougher. Then on again under granite bridges that are like moss and lichen rock-garden natural formations in a deep grotto, up the narrow quarry of the river where it hammers at its million-year-old boulders. And now he begins to feel one of those sensations that he liked, coming down from above: the atmospheric pressure – a high silence, a ghost-crowded emptiness, ancientness, eeriness – of wild moorland. Above the tangle of boughs, granite Dartmoor is beginning to lean in on him. The trout here are impossible to see in the hard-working water. If he could scare one under a rock, and feel for it there, and catch it and bring it out squirming in his grip, he'd be surprised to find himself holding a dark bronze, archaic-looking dagger of a fish, almost sooty bronze, corroded with blackish spots and red flecks. But he won't catch it. He'd be better to straighten his back and look up ahead, thinking he's only about half a mile to go – and then be really startled. Not surprised – startled.

The white shape of Gidleigh Park Hotel never fails to be startling, when you come on it suddenly like that. And there's no other way of coming on it except suddenly. If you've driven from Chagford, and found the first encouraging Gidleigh Park Hotel sign, and nosed your way into the alarmingly narrow lane, and twisted carefully through all its perverse twists, climbing and plunging, more and more alarmed as the maze grows more and more burrow-like, between walls of granite fortifications levered and inched into place by incredibly strong Trolls, or by teams of badgers maybe, and tied in with ferns and flowers, the dark river reappearing and disappearing, you imagine you're entering Merlin's kingdom not much changed, and you're ready for anything when suddenly – you swing into the open. And there it is.

Whether you arrive in the daylight and see it there, slightly lifted, under the steep woods, afloat on its terraces and gardens, above the cascades of the river, or arrive after nightfall and suddenly see it like a long, lit ship at anchor in a cove under the dark bulk of Dartmoor – your expectations soar.

The more you're aware of these approaches, the better. This magical, otherworld setting of Gidleigh Park – part Elfland studded with prehistoric prayer stones, sacrifice stones, vision stones, misted and draped with flowers according to season, partly last stronghold of the Celtic Dumnoni, who mustered their shaggy gods here against the Romans, then against the Saxons, then against the Norsemen, and partly the salmon-killing place of the bears – is important. It's important for the mood – which is the fantasy life of the palate.

Once you step inside, everything intensifies, by contrast. Paul Henderson and his wife Kay, the proprietors, are perfectionists on the heroic scale. Wide easy spaces recede beyond open doorways, depth beyond depth of comfort and privacy. At the right time of year, big log fires. By day, through the great windows, you look down over the terraces and the river gardens, into a widening valley vista hacked by the river out of a mountain range once as high as the Himalayas, but now carpeted, in the foreground, beyond a flower meadow, with the Stockey Furzon croquet lawn, levelled to the eighth of an inch.

But your pleasures are barely tasted yet. If Paul and Kay Henderson are the Arthur and Guinevere of this spellbinding kingdom (and they must have a magic touch, the morale of their staff is another of the invisible delights) the real Merlin is Shaun Hill.

The setting is as magical as it is, actually, because it has such a magician. Seeing all this, and entering it with your fantasy at full stretch, wildly hopeful, you do think – if this place has the right chef it will be too good to be true.

Not even Keats would have found the just phrases for Shaun Hill's cooking. Food writers who have made his style famous on two continents can only point towards the range, brilliance and delicacy of his dishes. Absolutely fresh food of the most select quality, fanatic daily routines of cleanliness in the kitchen, an artistic curiosity that searches constantly and voraciously through the great restaurants of the Western World, an unusually high IQ and critical wit – none of these explains the unique and consistent balance of pleasures that he sets before the guests at Gidleigh Park. Words are not the medium for what it is that makes all the difference.

But Keats would, for sure, identify the staple ingredients. He appreciated simplicity, naturalness, honesty, freshness, and he would be the keenest to luxuriate in the thronging of subtleties that haunt along the edges of every flavour – he recognised the art that conceals art.

He would have noticed, too, that food here has evolved in a special way. Those flavours carry something of the spanking newness and glitter of the Teign, whose voice whispers into every corner of the hotel, and it is not easy to separate them from a half awareness of the granite tors, sculpted and smoothed by the winds of aeons, and the granite stumps of hut circles, nursed into place and positioned by man's hand, up on the moor overhead, or from the electrical presences that flicker and glance around these ancient woods, and strange rocks, under the fifty-million-year-old skyline. The spirit of the place has had its effect on Shaun Hill.

Keats was susceptible to infatuation, and he might well have spent his annuity coming here. He knew how many million years he was going to be non-existent ('O for a life of sensations rather than thoughts!'). And it's certain, as a fire-eating gourmet, he would have found a soulmate in his equally curly, equally Celtic cousin Shaun Hill. And no doubt he would say, as I have several times heard after a Shaun Hill dinner: 'Every time I come here, I have the conviction that it's been possibly the best meal I've ever had. Am I under a spell?'

Then Shaun Hill would probably answer: 'Maybe Paul's wine list helped'.

But Keats would be murmuring extempore:

> When you lift up your eyes
> From History's cries
> Shaun Hill can prepare a Red Mullet
> To soothe your birth
> On this wink of an earth
> And immortalise your gullet.
>
> Bring Sweetbreads and Lamb in
> Defiance of Famine
> To bloom on your dish like a flower!
> Call Salmon and Sole
> To Shaun Hill in a shoal
> And he'll give them their finest hour.
>
> God's boldest creation
> Was the elation
> Of Adam and Eve on their gallops –
> Then He gave them Gidleigh
> Saying: 'Go and get tiddly
> Over Shaun Hill's Coriander and Scallops'.

Ted Hughes, Poet Laureate,
May 1990.

INTRODUCTION

My route to Gidleigh Park has been quite circuitous for I have no family history of working with food or wine, just the imbibing and appreciation of it. As a chef, my background and training ranged from the eclecticism of Robert Carrier in the early seventies, through the robust flavours of Middle European cooking and the classic French kitchen. A more important influence, however, in recent years, has been the continuing ease of access to good ingredients and the possibilities they open. The isolation of Gidleigh Park – for it is in a remote corner of Devon, next to Dartmoor – has allowed me to synthesise my cooking experience in an English country landscape, and I do believe that the setting with its rugged scenery and sparse population has had an impact on the type of dishes I cook.

Gidleigh Park was started in 1977 and is still run by an American couple, Kay and Paul Henderson. They liked food, ate out extensively, and wanted to create the sort of hotel that they would like to stay at themselves. Initially Kay cooked and Paul badgered the guests. He and I met during the period when Gidleigh was starting to achieve some real success. In 1979 I was cooking at Blake's Hotel where he was a regular customer. We kept in touch over the years and then in 1985, with my own restaurant more popular with the *Good Food Guide* than Barclay's Bank, we decided to join forces.

Curiously, I think it is customers like the Hendersons who have led the food revolution in England. The increase in disposable income of the middle classes has created within a generation a restaurant clientele who demand high standards. Some of them were free of the history of awful school food forced down the throats of the upper classes who used to comprise almost the whole eating-out public. Contrary to some so-called expert opinion, the chain stores have looked to restaurants for sophisticated dishes which are taken into the homes of these restaurant clients. The beauty of today's British audience is its receptiveness to new and different ideas and techniques. It is ironic that people lacking a base of skilled home cooking accept readily Indian, Chinese and now Thai food.

For in Britain, true regional cuisine, if it ever lived, is dead. We draw our inspiration from France, Italy, America and Asia. Our mothers did not bring us up on perfect *pot au feu* – more likely fish fingers and chicken curry. But the English public are evolving into demanding and knowledgeable customers, whose wine awareness and interest shame their French counterparts. The French undoubtedly have one of the finest food cultures in the world, but it is bound in a corset of rules and traditions, and by no means covers the entire spectrum of cooking possibilities; witness the nasty results of using uncooked curry powder mixed with white sauce in some quite celebrated restaurants.

In England, though, the technique of the chef is almost certainly more questionable than the quality of the produce. A piece of oxtail beautifully prepared over a few hours is worth just as much as a piece of Scottish beef fillet dropped on a grill. At home I cook tripe, brains, tongue, and the like, and would love to bring more of this cooking into the restaurant – and surely will as more clients are ready to accept and enthuse over them.

I like to cook, to eat, and of course to see the reactions of customers who like food. Not so much on their faces, but from the way the plates are returned to the kitchen, which reveals clearly the enthusiasm or lack of it with which the dish was received. Cooking is not an end in itself, though, but the route to a meal. Professionals often lose sight of this; chefs and managers don't eat out often enough themselves. I don't think you can understand the preparation of good food unless you know how to eat, enjoy eating, and enjoy the interplay of wine or beer with food. Catering people often make the worst customers in restaurants, having really come to compare cutlery and menu choice to their own establishments, or to put a stopwatch on the time between courses. They seem to enjoy themselves about as much as away football supporters actually enjoy watching the skills of the players.

And so to the book. Written for pleasure, to be used, I hope, as I have used the books that inspired me. It won't compare to the magic I felt when first reading Elizabeth David, but if any of her enthusiasm for food, for actually touching it and eating it, appears in my book it will be worthwhile. Cooking is at best an inexact science, and sometimes presented as too much of an art. For me it is a pleasure, and I hope you agree.

Menu planning

If you are planning a dinner party, build it around the course that is most important to you – generally the main course. See the meal as an entity; use cream in one course only. Chefs and domestic cooks alike over-use cream, butter and alcohol; this is expensive, unhealthy and unnecessary.

Do not become obsessive: remember, taste is everything, and try not to allow thoughts about colour to get in the way. Do not be hidebound by the traditional structures: there is no logical reason why the main course should be bigger than the starter. People these days are often happy with a series of light courses and prefer not to be overburdened by heaving platters of meat and vegetables.

There are no fixed rules. Pastry in more than one course is unimaginative and too much work. As a general rule you would not follow a hot starter with a cold main course, but this is not sacrosanct. When you are planning your menu look at it from the consumer's side. Would you really want to eat it, or will it go with the wine you have available? Beware of bullying ingredients like chillies, cream, brandy and garlic; these should be used with restraint and taste. Bread should be an integral part of the meal, not an afterthought.

If you are serving foie gras get some brioche or potato bread; *bresaola* is a perfect starter matched with an olive oil bread.

As much as you vary your ingredients and would not serve chicken followed by chicken, vary your methods. Do not have one pan-fried ingredient followed by another. Introduce slow-cooked items into your repertoire. This also enables you to sit down with your guests. Be aware that clean, sharp tastes encourage you to eat, and try not to follow a solid starter with a more solid main course. The pace of the meal is important too: ideally twenty minutes between the starter and the main course.

Make sure that your guests have food and drink freely available on arrival. People will arrive hungry, so give some time to the snacks that will receive them – some home-made cheese biscuits perhaps, or morsels of smoked salmon. Time spent on this is better spent than on intricate petits-fours. Do not be afraid to not offer a wide choice of drinks. Wine, particularly from Alsace or the Loire, is a perfect aperitif; do not try to serve champagne right through dinner, and don't hesitate to serve your best wine first while everyone's palate is awake. You can also serve red wine before white wine though this can be seen as unusual. Always make sure that you think of food and wine together. The food and wine will be in your mouth and stomach together, so see them as component parts of a whole, not two competing elements.

A dinner party should not try to reflect a restaurant. Too many chefs fail to see the point of a menu; it is there to communicate what is on offer, not to enhance your status by being in French or by using meaningless and recherché culinary terms. Equally, your dinner party is to feed and please your guests. As a general rule, fat people make better guests and you are better off with the greedy and over-indulgent. So first check your guests, and if they are laden down with allergies send them to hospital. The perfect dinner party needs enthusiastic and tolerant guests, and a host who is using good taste, skill and restraint, not trying to show off.

Henri Gault, author of the famous restaurant guides, says if you are offered a sorbet between courses, put on your coat and go home. This might be a bit extreme in English society but there is certainly no need to inflict misguided restaurant habits on people who are guests at your home. For your guests to enjoy themselves, you must take account of price, time, storage, space, facilities, crockery and cutlery. You must be sure that you can give enough time; do not make salads in the afternoon. Do not have a fridge full of dishes that will end up tasting like a fridge.

Like everything else, give it your best shot, which should carry you through the evening. One thing you should ask your guests is to comment on the food openly, not allowing them to be ashamed or embarrassed by their thoughts. It should not be intellectualised, but it should certainly be allowed pride of place. If they hate it, they should say so, but more importantly, if they like it, they should say so, for that is the point of being a cook.

1

SOUPS AND VEGETABLES

There is a Cinderella quality to the making of soups and preparation of vegetable dishes. They don't receive much thought or attention. Yet they should. When vegetables are not doing duty around some piece of meat or fish, both they and soups inhabit the early stages of the meal when palates are still fresh and receptive to interesting and complex flavours. More than anywhere else it is here your cooking should sparkle; it's always wise to put your best shots in early before the volume of food eaten and wine consumed take their toll.

Soups

Soup-making and sauce-making are related skills. Perversely sauce-making has an elevated status in cookery, reflecting all the kitchen's prestige, whereas soups have all but disappeared from the menu. Could it be that soup's peasant overtones or its image as a vehicle for leftovers may be inconsistent with restaurant prices?

Most soups are stock based. In some, like *minestrone*, the contributing ingredients will remain suspended in the stock; in others they may be blended to thicken the soup as purée. Classier soups may be clarified with egg white to make consommé and then thickened with a liaison of cream and egg yolks.

By definition, in making a soup you are transforming the texture of most ingredients to liquid. This gives you an unbelievable opportunity to create complex and successful dishes. The nutty taste of morel mushrooms with asparagus, almonds with chicken, and leek with potato are good examples. As in everything show restraint. Too many contrasts and clashes will create confusion in a dish that should be blended in perfect harmony. Also use restraint with cream, and if you find that you have created a dull cream soup, then a squeeze of lemon juice or a dash of wine vinegar may liven it up.

Don't use soup to tidy up leftovers unless they happen to add something you want to the end result. If you don't wish to eat your kitchen scraps, I'm afraid you have to put them in the dustbin or feed them to the birds.

Vegetables

Cookery has not yet risen to the challenge of vegetables. No area of food produce has changed so dramatically over the last 15 years as the availability of vegetables and fruit. Bunched carrots and turnips, asparagus and courgettes are all readily available all year round.

Don't be snooty about these imports. I live in the countryside and don't need to be told how superior fresh lifted new potatoes are to their Egyptian or Cypriot counterparts; we grow and cut our own asparagus and broad beans in early summer. But what about the winter? Non-stop brassica and frost-damaged potatoes, no thanks.

Vegetables are no longer cheap. It is my hope that they become even more expensive so that, like fish, they can no longer be treated with so little respect.

A good start would be to separate them from their traditional role as bridesmaid to the main-course meat. An individual course of carefully thought-about vegetables and perhaps a handful of wild mushrooms could transform your ideas of menu planning.

THAI SOUP

The inspiration for this dish comes not from a visit to Bangkok or the Thai restaurants which have proliferated in Britain in recent years, but from Ann and Franco Taruschio at the Walnut Tree Inn at Abergavenny. After adopting their Thai daughter, they travelled regularly to Thailand, and Ann particularly has learned many of their cooking skills.

There are quite a few unusual ingredients in this soup, some of which need careful handling. Coconut milk is normally only available tinned or dried in packets. We use the foil packets of white powder which come with instructions for reconstitution as thin, medium or thick. For this dish, you want the thin variety.

Lemongrass is a fibrous bulb about the size of a spring onion. The flavour becomes less pronounced from the base up the stalk. Its flavour is completely distinctive – break open the base, take a good sniff, and you could be addicted to its fresh, herby aroma.

Galangal is related to ginger and looks rather like it, but tastes different. It was known in England in the Middle Ages, and has a reputation as an aphrodisiac – good luck. Galangal powder is an acceptable substitute.

Nam Pla is produced commercially by several companies. It is a sauce made from anchovies that have been salted and fermented in the open air for several days. It is to Thai cooking what soy sauce is to Chinese, and like soy it is quite salty, so you won't need any more salt in the soup.

The coriander *must* be fresh, dried won't do at all. Lime leaves are very fragrant, but beware the stems which are as thorny as any bramble.

These ingredients are now widely available in Chinatown and other Asian shops. The best time to buy fresh ingredients is Friday morning, when the weekly ingredients arrive by air freight from Bangkok. We get everything from the wonderfully named emporium, Mata Hari Stores, in Earl's Court.

Serves 4

½ chicken, boned and cut into bite-sized pieces
6 stalks lemongrass
8 oz (225 g) galangal, or 2 teaspoons Laos or Ka powder
4 oz (100 g) lime leaves
3 spring onions, finely chopped
2 small fresh chillies, finely chopped
2 pints (1.2 litres) coconut milk
juice of 3 limes
1 tablespoon Nam Pla
2 tablespoons chopped coriander leaves

1. Place the chicken and a pint (600 ml) of water in a saucepan.
2. Cut the lemongrass into ½ in (1 cm) lengths. Trim off as much of the galangal skin as you wish, a little left will do no harm. Bruise both lemongrass and galangal with the flat of a heavy knife to release flavour, and add them to the pot. Wash and add the lime leaves.
3. Bring to the boil and simmer for half an hour. The chicken should be cooked but still tender, and the other ingredients should have released their flavours. Remove from the heat.
4. Add the spring onion and chillies. Remove the chicken, dice the breast meat, and keep it for garnish. Also cut up the leg meat, and keep it for later.
5. Add the coconut milk and squeeze the limes into the mixture. Limes will give more juice if you press them with your fingers before squeezing.
6. Bring the soup to the boil again for a few seconds, add the Nam Pla, remove from the heat and strain. (Thin coconut milk will split if you boil it too long.) Add the reserved chicken meat from the legs, and liquidise the mixture.
7. Add the diced chicken breast meat and the coriander, reheat and serve.

PHEASANT AND LENTIL SOUP

Pheasant is good value. The majority of the cost of breeding and raising these birds is recouped from those who pay to shoot them, a strange arrangement but one from which the cook benefits.

The stronger flavour of a well-hung bird suits this soup which is gently spicy. It is probably more sensible to make double the quantity and freeze half – that way you will use the whole pheasant. Of course, you may like the soup enough to drink two bowlfuls each!

Serves 4

1.   Soak the lentils in cold water for at least an hour. Look them over carefully for any little stones or grit. Boil in plenty of salted water for 10 minutes, then drain.

2.   Take all the pheasant meat off the bone and keep it to one side. Peel the carrot and onion, then chop them finely. Fry the bones, carrot peelings and any oddments from the onion with half the butter in a saucepan until brown. Pour on 2 pints (1.2 litres) of water and bring to the boil. Simmer for 10 minutes and then turn off the heat. When this has cooled decant the stock into a clean jug for use a little later.

3.   Take a medium-sized saucepan and warm the remaining butter in it. Fry the onion and carrot with the garlic and ginger for 5 minutes until they start to colour. Add the leg meat from the pheasant and all the spices.

4.   Let them fry for a few seconds before adding the tomatoes, two-thirds of the lentils and two-thirds of the pheasant stock. Bring to the boil then simmer for 20 minutes.

5.   Liquidise the soup in a blender, then pass it through a fine sieve. Check the flavour. You will need salt, pepper and lemon juice to counter the alkaline flavours of the large amount of mild spices used. Add the lemon juice in drops until the balance is right.

2 oz (50 g) brown lentils
½ pheasant
salt
1 carrot
1 medium onion
1½ oz (40 g) unsalted butter
1 garlic clove, peeled and crushed
1 small knob ginger, peeled and chopped
3 cinnamon sticks
1 tablespoon coriander seeds, crushed
½ fresh nutmeg, grated
freshly ground black pepper
2 tomatoes, de-seeded
a little lemon juice

To complete
a few sprigs of flat parsley, chopped
1 tablespoon double cream

To complete

6.   Heat the remaining stock. Poach the breast meat until just cooked, but still moist, about 15 minutes. Lift out the meat with a slotted spoon, slice it thinly and divide between four warmed soup bowls along with the remaining lentils and the chopped parsley.

7.   Add this stock to the soup, and heat. Add a little cream, no more than a tablespoonful, to improve the texture. As it comes to the boil pour into the garnished bowls.

Once puréed, the soup shouldn't have prolonged boiling or the texture will turn grainy.

CHICKPEA AND LANGOUSTINE SOUP

Chickpeas need to soak for two days in cold water, so this is no spur-of-the-moment soup. Baking soda is supposed to help tenderise the peas as they soak, and a pinch may be added to the water. Allow generous amounts of time when cooking chickpeas. They are indigestible if underdone and almost impossible to overcook.

I ate soups like this one in northern Italy recently. After a day's driving, and having been constantly flashed and hooted at by the natives, a soothing and delicious meal was important to restore mental equilibrium. A holiday driving in Italy is akin to a holiday windsurfing round Cape Horn, not for those of a nervous disposition. Good dishes like this along with liberal quantities of Gaja's and Antinori's wines seemed to make it feel worthwhile.

Serves 4

8 oz (225 g) chickpeas
4 langoustines
salt
2 tablespoons extra virgin olive oil
1 large onion, peeled and sliced
2 large garlic cloves, peeled and sliced
1 teaspoon coriander seeds, crushed
juice of ½ lemon
freshly ground black pepper

To complete
2 tablespoons extra virgin olive oil

1.   Soak the chickpeas for 2 days, then drain them. Bring to the boil in 2 pints (1.2 litres) of lightly salted – a pinch only – water and simmer until tender. This will take at least 2 hours and may take double.
2.   Blend the chickpeas together with their cooking liquor in a liquidiser.
3.   Heat the olive oil in a shallow pan, and fry the onion and garlic until they start to colour. Add the crushed coriander seeds and the langoustines. When the langoustines start to give a cooked smell, maybe 2 minutes, pour in 10 fl oz (300 ml) water and bring to the boil.
4.   About 2 minutes later lift out the langoustines and remove the tail meat for use as garnish in the finished soup. Return the bones and debris to the pan and cook for a further 5 minutes.
5.   Strain this liquor into a clean saucepan and add to it the chickpea purée. You will need to adjust the balance of flavour with lemon juice, black pepper and a little more salt. The soup should be fairly thick. If it is too thick, let it down with some water or stock.

To complete

6.   Bring the soup to the boil and ladle into warmed soup bowls. Chop the langoustine meat and sprinkle it on top. Finish the soup by pouring ½ tablespoonful of finest, extra virgin olive oil on to each bowlful.

LEEK AND SAFFRON SOUP

We used to make this soup when I worked at Carrier's restaurant in Islington. It isn't difficult, and was often the *commis* cook's job.

If you didn't already know, Robert Carrier was a major influence in the awakening of public interest in food in the sixties. He wrote regularly in the *Sunday Times* and managed to draw into his columns much of the tone and feel of the Mediterranean, so that his recipes seemed part of an alluring travelogue rather than mere ingredient lists.

At the time, it was a brave move for him to open a restaurant. He had advocated a definite approach to food in his writing, and was a target for bitchy sniping, some from competitor journalists, and some from people he had miffed in his articles. It was certainly one of Britain's best restaurants in its day, and I learned a lot there.

Carrier didn't cook, but compiled the menu and dictated the style. It was a good arrangement for the cooks, because we knew very little outside the classical repertoire. None of us had heard of *satay*, or lamb in Greek pastry, nor even French *bourgeois* dishes like *boeuf à la ficelle*.

We made few soups in the restaurant. This was my favourite, and we had it at home adding mussels or chicken leftovers to make it more of a meal. The quantities are sufficient for eight people. It's not worth making less, and you can freeze it before the cream is added.

Serves 8

8 oz (225 g) chicken winglets
1 lb (450 g) leeks
8 oz (225 g) potatoes
1 medium onion
1 celery stalk
⅛ oz (5 g) saffron
2 fl oz (50 ml) white wine
salt and freshly ground black
  pepper

To complete
2 egg yolks
4 fl oz (120 ml) double cream

1.   Roast the chicken winglets in a hot oven – say, 400°F (200°C) Gas 6 – until they start to colour, about 20 minutes. Lift them from the roasting tray into a saucepan. Deglaze the roasting tray by adding a little water and bringing to the boil. This will extract the chicken flavour, in the same way as gravy making, from the tray. Pour this into the saucepan with the winglets, along with 2½ pints (1.5 litres) water.
2.   Bring this to the boil and simmer for about 20 minutes.
3.   Lift the winglets from the stock. Separate the meat from the bones, and return the meat to the stock.
4.   Cut the leeks into 1 in (2.5 cm) pieces. Peel and cube the potatoes to the same size. Peel and chop the onion and the celery stalk. Wash them all in plenty of cold water.
5.   Add the vegetables and the saffron to the stock. Put a lid on the pan, and cook until tender, about 40 minutes.
6.   Liquidise the soup base in a blender.
7.   Add the white wine, and carefully adjust the seasoning. You will need plenty of salt because of the potato.

To complete

8.   To finish the soup, mix the egg yolks and cream in a bowl. Pour a cupful of soup on to this mixture and whisk them together, then return this to the saucepan and stir it in.
9.   Serve immediately. Do not re-boil or the egg and cream liaison will curdle.

Asparagus and Wild Mushroom Soup

This soup should taste fresh so try not to cook the asparagus too long. Asparagus and wild mushrooms are not in season simultaneously although they are both widely available, so this soup will never have a feeling of being traditional. The two ingredients marry together well, however, and we cannot be blamed for the inadequacies of our ancestors' supply and distribution networks.

The vegetables

Serves 4

1 lb (450 g) asparagus
½ oz (15 g) dried morel
    mushrooms
1 small leek
groundnut oil
8 oz (225 g) chicken winglets

To complete
salt and freshly ground black
    pepper
1 egg yolk
1 fl oz (25 ml) double cream
a little lemon juice

1.   Peel the asparagus from just below the tip down to the base, and keep the peelings. Cut off and discard the bases of the stems which are woody and often have mould spores which taint the soup. Slice the stems into ¼ in (6 mm) pieces, and keep the tips intact because they look nice in the soup.
2.   Soak the dried morels for an hour in cold water, then cut them in half lengthwise and wash out any grit.
3.   Trim, top and tail the leek. Cut into ½ in (1 cm) lengths and wash well.

The soup

4.   Use a saucepan with a heavy base that you can fry and boil in. Heat it and add a few drops of the groundnut oil, then put in the chicken winglets and leek. Let these brown, moving them about the pot regularly so that they don't stick. Pour in 2½ pints (1.5 litres) of cold water.
5.   Bring this to the boil, and drop in the asparagus tips and morels. Let them boil for 2 minutes and then take them out with a slotted spoon. Run a little cold water on the asparagus to arrest the cooking and preserve the colour. Put the asparagus tips and morels aside until later.
6.   Let the broth simmer for 20 minutes, then add the sliced asparagus stems and peelings. Do not let them boil for more than 2 minutes or the fresh asparagus flavour will be lost, and you might as well have used tinned.
7.   Remove from the heat and decant into a container. Pick the chicken meat from the bones. Liquidise with the broth and the asparagus trimmings.

To complete

All the preceding work can be done in advance. Once you have moved from this point you must serve the soup, and it can only be reheated if you are *very, very* careful.

8.   Toss the blanched asparagus tips and morels in a few drops of groundnut oil. Season with salt and pepper.
9.   Mix the egg yolk and cream in a cup or bowl and pour in a little soup. Mix together to form a liaison. If necessary, reheat the soup, pour the liaison into it and stir well. Turn off the heat.
10.   Season with salt until it tastes right. Add a squeeze of lemon. Strain into bowls and float the morels and asparagus tips on top of each bowl.

Ragout of Wild Mushrooms and Baby Vegetables

This dish has no formal set of ingredients, and what I give you is a guideline. It should be entirely seasonal, a combination of what is best at the market.

The trade in baby vegetables has turned a little silly recently. Cauliflowers and cabbage are no better small than normal sized, just a lot more expensive. But do not be put off by this trendy bandwagon: baby carrots and leeks are exquisite.

Serves 4

8 baby artichokes
salt
juice of ½ lemon
2 tomatoes
1 bunch baby carrots
4 oz (100 g) slender French
  beans
4 oz (100 g) mange-touts
4 baby leeks
8 small asparagus spears
8 oz (225 g) broad beans
8 oz (225 g) mixed wild
  mushrooms (chanterelles,
  morels, black trumpets, etc)
a knob of unsalted butter

To complete
5 fl oz (150 ml) double cream

1.   Cut the outer leaves from the artichokes, then trim down to the choke (see page 22). Boil in salted water and the lemon juice to cover, about 20 minutes if they are small. Rinse in cold water then use a teaspoon to remove the hairy fibrous part from the middle.
2.   Skin the tomatoes by immersing in boiling water for 10 seconds and then peeling. Cut them into quarters and scrape away the seeds.
3.   Cut the greenery from the carrots and peel them (peel very thinly, or scrub very hard if they are really small). Top and tail the French beans, mange-touts and leeks. If you can't get baby asparagus, cut off the stalks of normal spears. Pod the broad beans and then drop the beans in boiling water for a few seconds. Refresh them in cold water and peel away their skins.
4.   Scrape as much grit as possible from the wild mushrooms, especially the morels, which often have little stones inside. At the last minute, wash the mushrooms in plenty of cold water and pat them dry with kitchen paper.
5.   Bring about 10 fl oz (300 ml) water to the boil in a good-sized saucepan. Salt the vegetables rather than the water. Put them into the water in the order they need to be cooked – carrots first, then leeks, then French beans and broad beans, peas and mange-touts last. The process shouldn't take more than about 7 or 8 minutes, and the mange-touts shouldn't cook more than a minute or two.
6.   Sauté the wild mushrooms with a little butter in a frying pan, about 3 minutes.

To complete

7.   Lift out the vegetables and mushrooms, and divide them between soup dishes with the tomato and artichokes.
8.   Boil the cooking liquor and the pan juices from the mushrooms together with the cream for a few minutes to amalgamate, and spoon this over the ragoût. Serve at once.

CHARCOAL-GRILLED VEGETABLES WITH TOMATO AND MARJORAM SAUCE

The vegetables for this dish are grilled from raw. They aren't part-boiled in advance. The sort of overhead grill most cookers have, which chefs know as a salamander, does not cook this dish properly. If you have a barbecue set in the garden shed, that would be perfect.

These grilled vegetables make a good first course. You would need to avoid duplicating the ingredients in your main course, naturally. Maybe give a tossed salad instead. The dish, without the tomato sauce, will partner any grilled meat and I use grilled vegetables with sirloin steak and Meaux mustard sauce on my own menu.

The grilling process leaves a line of black marks from the bars of the grill. I find this quite appealing but have come across people who assume the vegetables have been burnt or carelessly cooked. I am sure you would not allow such silly people into your homes, however.

The sauce

Serves 4

12 tender young leeks
12 baby sweetcorn
12 young carrots from a bunch
12 baby turnips
12 small asparagus
2 tablespoons olive oil
salt and freshly ground black
  pepper

Sauce
2 lb (900 g) tomatoes
4 tablespoons olive oil
1 garlic clove, peeled and
  chopped
1 small onion, peeled and
  chopped
1 sprig fresh marjoram
1 teaspoon sugar

1.   Skin the tomatoes by dropping them in boiling water for 10 seconds and then peeling. Cut out the cores, de-seed them and then chop them finely.
2.   Warm the olive oil and then gently sauté the garlic and onion for 5 minutes so that they are cooked but not coloured.
3.   Add the tomato and the leaves from the sprig of marjoram. Let this simmer for 25 minutes until the sauce is no longer watery.
4.   Adjust the seasoning with sugar, black pepper and salt.

The vegetables

5.   Wash the vegetables and where necessary peel or trim them. Pat them thoroughly dry on kitchen paper and brush with olive oil. Season with salt and pepper.
6.   Grill the vegetables in the order of how much cooking time they need. First turnips, then carrots, then leeks, sweetcorn and asparagus.

Seal them in the hottest part of the grill, then let them cook a little more slowly on the cooler edges. Inevitably one or two outer leaves of the leeks will become too black. Just peel them away and discard them.

To complete

7.   Serve the vegetables hot with a couple of spoonfuls of the tomato and marjoram sauce.

The tomato and marjoram mixture is not sieved or liquidised like a pukka sauce. You can, of course, blend it if you prefer.

ARTICHOKE NISSARDA

In concept, at least, this is a reasonably simple vegetable dish which makes a good starter. It is an artichoke heart filled with mushroom stuffing and coated with hollandaise sauce. If you didn't know, hollandaise sauce is an emulsion of butter and egg yolks. It isn't difficult but does need patience and the judicious control of heat so that the egg yolks cook without scrambling.

My colleague Richard Shepherd, who was the first head chef at the Capital Hotel in London, collected this recipe whilst working in southern France. It has always been amongst my favourites.

The mushroom stuffing

1. Put the shallots and mushrooms into a food processor and chop them until fine but not a purée.
2. Place this stuffing into a small saucepan with the olive oil, a pinch of salt and some pepper. Stir to the boil, then fit a lid and simmer for 10–15 minutes. Take care that the stuffing doesn't burn for it dries out as it cooks.

The artichokes

3. Artichokes seem to produce twice the volume of trimmings to their original bulk. Arrange a small production line with, first, a dustbin over which to trim the artichokes, next a small bowl with most of the lemon juice, and lastly the saucepan in which you will cook them. This should contain some cold water, salt, dried herb and a few drops of lemon juice.

Snap off the stalks and discard them. With a short serrated knife (any good bread knife will do), slice a thin layer from the base and sides. Then cut off the top of the artichoke leaving about 1 in (2.5 cm) of base. You will now need a small sharp knife, like a cook's turning knife, to trim away the rest of the leaves and any bristly or green patches. Work delicately as you do this or you will lose some of the artichoke bottom.

4. As you finish each 'choke drop it into the lemon juice and then into the saucepan. Boil with a tight-fitting lid until tender, about 20 minutes, depending on the size of the vegetables.
5. Take a spoon and carefully scrape out the hairy fibres from the centre of the 'choke.

The hollandaise sauce

6. Clarify the butter by heating it slowly in a saucepan so that the butter oil separates and rises to the top.
7. Whisk the egg yolks and 2 fl oz (50 ml) water over a low heat until you have a cooked sabayon, a texture that is thick yet light and creamy. Off the heat, whisk in the clarified butter a spoonful at a time. The butter and egg

Serves 4

4 large artichokes
juice of 1 lemon
1 teaspoon dried oregano
salt and freshly ground black
  pepper

Mushroom stuffing
2 oz (50 g) shallots, peeled and
  sliced
4 oz (100 g) button mushrooms,
  washed and sliced
1 teaspoon olive oil

Hollandaise sauce
3 oz (75 g) unsalted butter
2 egg yolks
lemon juice
a pinch of cayenne pepper

yolk sabayon should be at a similar temperature. Finish the sauce with some lemon juice, salt and cayenne pepper.

To complete

8.   Place one artichoke heart on each plate. Place a spoonful of mushroom stuffing in the centre and then coat with hollandaise sauce.

GRILLED MARINATED TOFU AND SWEET PEPPERS WITH SAFFRON SAUCE

Tofu is a bland soya curd which many regard as a practical joke played by science and Mother Nature on vegetarians. However it can be a surprisingly adept vehicle for interesting flavours, having so little of its own, and can provide a useful contrast of texture in vegetable dishes.

I would serve this dish with pilaff rice, a good green salad and warm buttermilk rolls (see page 106). Should you feel like adding other vegetables like courgettes, so much the better.

Serves 4

1 lb (450 g) tofu
2 red peppers
2 yellow peppers

Tofu marinade
10 fl oz (300 ml) olive oil
2 garlic cloves, peeled and
   crushed
1 sprig each of fresh thyme,
   parsley and marjoram
2 tablespoons wine vinegar
2 tablespoons Dijon mustard
salt and freshly ground black
   pepper

Saffron sauce
5 fl oz (150 ml) dry cider
⅛ oz (5 g) saffron
2 fl oz (50 ml) double cream

The tofu marinade

1.   Warm the oil with the crushed garlic and the thyme. Chop and add the other herbs, and let the oil cool. Whisk the vinegar and mustard together and, of course, salt and pepper. Then blend in the strained oil drop by drop. It should form a dressing-like emulsion.
2.   Cut the tofu into 1 in (2.5 cm) cubes and turn them in the marinade. Leave this overnight.
3.   Split the peppers and discard any pith and seeds. Cut into 1 in (2.5 cm) squares, and add briefly to the marinade.

To complete

4.   Thread pepper and tofu squares alternately on to skewers and then grill, preferably on a charcoal or wood barbecue, until well coloured on each side, about 5 minutes.
5.   Meanwhile, for the sauce, boil the dry cider and saffron together. Add cream and then, off the heat, whisk in what is left of the marinade. Warm through.
6.   Slip the kebabs off the skewers on to warmed plates, serve and eat straightaway, with the sauce.

Sea Kale with Morels and Butter Sauce

Sea kale – *Cramba maritima* – is a native English vegetable still growing wild near some sea shores. It isn't yet cultivated widely but is available, forced like rhubarb, in late winter. With its delicate flavour and exquisite crisp texture this vegetable is an aristocrat like asparagus.

Sea kale has been neglected in the past but is now grown commercially in Brittany and is available in Britain via the Paris market at the end of February and during March. The inevitable insult will be its resurgence of popularity as that French delicacy *'la crambe maritime'*.

Kale is anyway a misnomer, this being no brassica. Beware market men selling Swiss chard under the same name. Once separated from sprouts and cauli or new favourites kiwifruit and pawpaw, large sections of the greengrocery trade tend to become confused.

The vegetables

1. Sea kale looks and handles like fragile celery with white brittle stems joined at the base. These will need separating and careful washing. The stems are usually about 9 in (23 cm) long. If your plates are small or your saucepan inadequate, cut these stems into smaller lengths. Boil in plenty of salted water for 5 or 6 minutes. The stems are not at all tough so you don't need to cook them until tender unless you particularly like them that way.

2. Fresh morels are available at the same time as sea kale. If you are using dried then bring them to the boil in a small saucepan of water and allow to cool. Carefully wash away the inevitable grit. Only the caps are useable and they are easier to clean split in half. Melt the butter and fry the morels.

The butter sauce

3. Reduce the white wine by half in a small saucepan. Lower the heat and then whisk in the butter, piece by piece. Finish the sauce with lemon juice, salt and pepper. It should taste buttery but not greasy.

To complete

4. Drain the sea kale well. Too much retained moisture will dilute the butter sauce. Pour on the warm sauce and then add the nutty-tasting fried morels.

If morels are beyond budget, use a few chopped herbs or even plain lemon and butter.

Serves 4

2 sea kale
2 oz (50 g) morel mushrooms
1 oz (25 g) unsalted butter

Sauce
5 fl oz (150 ml) dry white wine
8 oz (225 g) unsalted butter, cut
  in pieces
juice of ½ lemon
salt and freshly ground black
  pepper

GRATIN DE JABRON

This is the best *gratin dauphinoise* potato I have tasted and was a regular accompaniment to rack of lamb and rib of beef at the Capital Hotel in London when I worked there. It came via Pierre Gleize, an early adviser to the Capital, who owns and cooks at La Bonne Étape in south-eastern France.

The dish is a course on its own. It is creamy and garlicky and yet doesn't lose the flavour of potato. If you have a choice, use potatoes that aren't too floury. They will hold together better when cooked.

I have split the recipe into two stages because that is how I cook it, preparing most of the dish in advance. You may, of course, proceed directly from the first to the second stage if you prefer. The grated cheese is optional and I now use it less often, especially when the gratin is to partner meat.

Jabron potatoes converted my Uncle Frank to garlic. A conservative in dress and taste, he associated garlic only with the breath and armpit smells of the rush-hour London Underground as it lurches from north to west across the city. As a proper Englishman he was convinced that it was garlic which differentiated our island race from the wops. Imagine his surprise then at how good this very garlicky dish tastes and the realisation that the problems of Tottenham Court Road's tube station were not dietary – merely absence of deodorant and toothpaste.

Stage 1 (up to 1 day in advance)

Serves 4

Stage 1
2 lb (900 g) maincrop potatoes
6 oz (175 g) unsalted butter
3 garlic cloves, peeled and
  crushed
salt and freshly ground black
  pepper

Stage 2
10 fl oz (300 ml) milk
10 fl oz (300 ml) double cream
2 oz (50 g) hard cheese,
  preferably Cheddar or
  Gruyère, grated

1.   Wash and sort the potatoes. You are going to boil them in their skins so it will be an advantage if they are approximately the same size.
2.   Boil the potatoes until they are just cooked, perhaps even a fraction underdone. Drain the water. Peel off the skin and then cut the potatoes into thickish – ¼ in (6 mm) – slices.
3.   Melt the butter with the crushed garlic in a frying pan. Unless you have a really big pan you will probably need to do this exercise two or three times in a smaller one. When the butter is melted, and mixed with the garlic but not yet hot or sizzling, add the potatoes and toss them. The object is to coat the potato slices with the garlic butter, not to fry them. Season with salt and pepper and then spoon them into a container until needed.

Stage 2 (20 minutes before you eat)

4.   Spread the potato on to a pie dish about 1 in (2.5 cm) deep. Pour on the milk and cream. Sprinkle the cheese on top.
5.   Bake at 350°F (180°C) Gas 4 for 20 minutes.

WILD RICE PILAFF

Unlike standard rice varieties, wild rice will not stick together. It also takes longer to cook. An answer is to boil the rice until it is almost cooked and then add it to a little pilaff of brown rice. This way you retain the unique liquorice-like flavour and slightly chewy taste of wild rice in the neat, easily handled form of pilaff.

This is an accompaniment, fine with game or calf's kidney. To make it a vegetable course you need only add a few dried ceps (*porcini*) or morels to the cooking liquor.

1.   Boil the wild rice in salted water for half an hour. It will still be a little hard. Drain away the water. Leave the rice still hot to rest while you make the pilaff.
2.   Sweat the onion in olive oil for 3 or 4 minutes in a medium-sized saucepan.
3.   Add the brown rice and sweat this also for 5 minutes.
4.   Season the rice with salt and pepper, then add about 10 fl oz (300 ml) water (or stock if you have it), and re-boil.
5.   Turn down the heat and cover the saucepan. After 5 minutes stir in the wild rice.
6.   Cover the pan again, and let the rice cook until all the water has evaporated, about 20 minutes.

Serves 4

4 oz (100 g) wild rice
salt and freshly ground black
   pepper
1 small onion, peeled and
   chopped
1 tablespoon olive oil
4 oz (100 g) brown rice,
   preferably short-grain

2

PASTA, RICE AND SNACKS

One of the longest serving and probably one of the most futile arguments takes place between the Italians and the Chinese as to whether Marco Polo took pasta to China or returned with it to Italy. It is probably of little consequence any longer, but one thing that this old story shows is that pasta is an adaptable and very practical food. Once dried it has a longer life than bread, potatoes or its other rivals. Pasta machines give you unlimited flexibility and you get equal inspiration these days from Italy, America and France, whether you make it or buy it. You will encounter pasta in wild colours, flavoured with squid ink, paprika, artichoke, tomato, etc. Dry pasta is perfectly good for many dishes. It is easy to cook and produces a good texture; a quality dry pasta will be better than some of the poor fresh pasta that is available. If you do make your own, make it in small quantities as it only keeps for 24 hours; some varieties will freeze. Most people enjoy pasta dishes as they give the opportunity to use small fiddly ingredients like cockles, clams, etc., creating a dish which is greater than the sum of its parts.

Do not use too much sauce as a little goes much further than you would think. Equally do not drown everything in Parmesan, however freshly grated it might be, particularly if there is fish with the pasta. A home-made pasta dish could be as fast as opening a tin of soup. Boil the pasta in lots of salted water. Toss on a plate with olive oil, grated cheese and a few herbs.

Another dish which you can create quickly from your store cupboard is risotto. A simple risotto again with cheese can be quite wonderful, though more interesting variations made with red wine, vegetables or wild mushrooms can elevate this dish into something quite perfect. Risotto, of course, can be used as a garnish with a fish or meat dish and, contrary to popular belief, can be prepared in advance. You sauté onions and then the rice until it is translucent. You cook the first glass of wine in the normal way and then add another, allow the dish to rest and when it needs to be served reduce the wine with a ladleful of stock until it is done – then your risotto will be perfect.

Probably the most popular savoury dish in the world at the moment is the pizza, which rivals in England the chicken vindaloo for soaking up too much beer or merely filling a gap. As the Californians have shown, a pizza can be subtle, exciting and not necessarily stodgy. It should however be made to order and eaten straightaway.

Once you have mastered the techniques of making pastry, you have many variations to play with. Using only single cream, you can create a wonderful quiche, flavoured perhaps with spinach, cream or blue cheese. Simpler still is Welsh rarebit, where strong, mature Cheddar should be blended with mustard, egg yolk and Worcestershire sauce.

Sandwiches in general are much maligned and yet a 'BLT' is probably one of the world's great quick dishes. Basil and Mozzarella, tomato or Raclette and ham combine brilliantly. A steak sandwich where the meat is topped with creamed mushrooms and mustard works well, and chicken livers make a superb filling for a toasted sandwich.

A sandwich should be interesting enough to serve as lunch and taste of more than bread. Dismiss from your thoughts those puny crustless combinations of bread and dry meat or cheese. Practically anything which makes a good first course or salad will convert into sandwich filling.

Open sandwiches use – obviously – less bread and so can take more distinctly flavoured breads like rye or odd-shaped ones like the French *pain de campagne*. Beware of artistry interfering with practicality when making open sandwiches. I have eaten some which looked a treat but were impossible to negotiate without a knife and fork. You may end up with more on your lap than in your mouth.

Canapés, the classic kind made with small triangles of cold toast and covered with aspic, overcome this problem. Unfortunately they usually taste awful and have that fiddly, ponced-up look which really only suits sweeties or petits-fours. Sandwiches fall into the category of foods which are for eating rather than photographing.

Whether you are making a pizza, pasta, risotto or sandwich, you should be able to improve them with items from a carefully balanced store cupboard. There are certain things that no self-respecting eater should be without because you never know when hard work or a hangover will cause an outbreak of appetite. I would keep stocks of dried pasta, frozen chicken livers, truffle oil, light and heavy olive oil, mustard, Worcestershire sauce, pine kernels, Parmesan, Pecorino, sun-dried tomatoes and Tabasco.

Parsley Fettucine with Broad Beans and Creme Fraiche

You need lots of broad beans, by weight, for each portion. By the time five pounds are out of their pods you will be lucky to have one pound of beans left. Young broad beans are essential for this dish. Large beans need far more cooking and will taste coarse.

Serves 4

2 oz (50 g) flat leaf parsley
2 tablespoons olive oil

Pasta
4 oz (100 g) plain flour
1 medium egg
salt and freshly ground black
    pepper
2 tablespoons olive oil

Beans and sauce
5 lb (2.25 kg) broad beans in
    pod
4 fl oz (120 ml) crème fraîche
2 oz (50 g) Parmesan cheese,
    grated

1.   Blend the parsley with the olive oil and 2 tablespoons of water in a liquidiser. Divide this purée into two.
2.   Combine the flour, egg, a good pinch of salt, and one-half of the parsley purée. Knead until smooth. Rest for 2 hours (the dough – not yourself).
3.   Shell the beans. Some people prefer to wear gloves for this, as the juices will leave a little dark stain, especially in large beans. Drop them into boiling water for 2 minutes and then drain. Remove the skins. You should be left with a bright green, tender vegetable.
4.   Roll out the pasta dough, on a machine if you have one, into thin ribbons about ⅓ in (8 mm) wide.

To complete

5.   Boil the fettucine in salted water for 2 minutes and then drain, shaking off as much liquid as you can. Season with salt and pepper, then toss in the olive oil.

6.   Boil the crème fraîche, remaining parsley purée and grated Parmesan in a saucepan, then add the beans.
7.   Twirl a portion of fettucine with a large fork and place one on each hot plate. Spoon the sauce and beans around the pasta and serve immediately.

OPEN RAVIOLI WITH CHICKEN LIVER, LEMON AND GARLIC

The edges of ravioli are the problem. Unless you are very skilled and have several generations of Italian blood in your veins, the outer part will be double the thickness of the rest and will not cook as well.

Another problem with ravioli is that you can't fit enough filling into the centres for my taste – not unless you make them very large, one per portion. Trendy restaurants in northern Italy feature *ravioli aperti* which avoid these problems. This way of assembling the ravioli after the pasta is cooked is fine.

Chicken livers are one of the few genuine luxury ingredients which are not yet expensive. I enjoy applying the same skill and effort to cheaper ingredients and, in fact, once bought a restaurant in Stratford-upon-Avon to demonstrate that sophisticated flavours could be served to people not blessed with an expense account. This wasn't an entirely good idea and when I say 'bought', what I mean is Barclays Bank bought a restaurant and owned all the assets. I merely worked seven days a week to make the payments and was responsible for the debts.

In time there were a reasonable number of customers who thought the food and wine were good but I resented the hours spent on paperwork rather than cooking. This paperwork will tend to increase in the ratio to which your overdraft does and Her Majesty's Customs & Excise officers will come and visit you regularly if you don't fill in their forms and post them large cheques. Making these officers stand in the rain in the back yard by the rubbish for a while before treating them to a few well-chosen jibes was, in retrospect, probably a mistake but elated me at the time.

This chicken liver dish was typical of the dishes on the menu. I make my own pasta which is not difficult but if you can buy fresh pasta then the dish is very quick to prepare.

The ravioli paste

1.   Mix the flour and semolina in a bowl, and add the beaten egg, olive oil, salt and pepper. Knead to a smooth dough. Don't be afraid to add a few drops of water but if you use too much the pasta will become brittle. Rest the dough in the fridge for at least an hour.

The stock

2.   Heat a saucepan and add the olive oil. Add the chicken winglets immediately, otherwise the oil will smoke. Cook until brown, about 5 minutes, turning occasionally.

Serves 4

8 oz (225 g) chicken livers
1 tablespoon olive oil

Ravioli paste
3 oz (75 g) strong plain flour
1 oz (25 g) semolina
1 medium egg, beaten
1 teaspoon olive oil
salt and freshly ground black
   pepper

Stock
1 teaspoon olive oil
4 oz (100 g) chicken winglets
1 medium onion, peeled and
   chopped

Sauce
4 garlic cloves, peeled and
   crushed
1 oz (25 g) Pecorino cheese,
   grated
zest of 1 lemon, grated
1 fl oz (25 ml) double cream
a little grated nutmeg

3. Add the onion to the winglets. As it colours pour on a pint (600 ml) of cold water. Bring to the boil and simmer to reduce for about 40 minutes.
4. Strain the stock into a bowl. You should have about 10 fl oz (300 ml) of rather cloudy stock and some chicken winglets for your cat.

These jobs can be done as far in advance as you wish.

To roll and cook the pasta

5. If you have a hand-cranked pasta machine, roll it through three times, the final time at the second thinnest setting. Otherwise use a rolling pin which will do the job as well except that it will not be such a neat exercise.
6. Cut the pasta into whatever shapes you want. A pedestrian 2 in (5 cm) square suits me but if you want to amaze your guests with Christmas cracker shapes this is also acceptable.
7. Boil a saucepan with plenty, say 3 pints (1.75 litres), of salted water, then drop in the pasta squares. They cook almost immediately, certainly within a minute.
8. Drain. Even when cooked, pasta will stick, so lay the squares on a damp cloth or oiled tray side by side and keep them warm for the few minutes you need to complete the dish.

To complete

9. Carefully trim the chicken livers, cutting away any greenish patches which are bitter, and separate each liver into its two lobes. Heat one large or two medium frying pans. If the pan isn't hot or if it is too crowded, the livers will stick.
10. Fry the livers in the olive oil for about 2 minutes, so that they remain pink inside, and then spoon them out on to kitchen paper.
11. Pour the stock into the pan(s) and let it reduce for a few seconds. Add the crushed garlic, grated cheese, lemon zest and cream, with some black pepper and grated nutmeg to taste. The sauce should be beige in colour and not too creamy in texture.
12. Divide half the ravioli squares between four warmed plates. Place the livers and a few drops of sauce on top. Lay the remaining squares on the livers and spoon over the sauce.

OPEN RAVIOLI WITH SMOKED RICOTTA AND NUTMEG BUTTER

Any firm of fish or poultry smokers will put a Ricotta into the smoker for you. The rest is straightforward.

Serves 4

1. Roll out the ravioli paste as thinly as possible and cut into 2 in (5 cm) squares. Boil for a few seconds in salted water and drain.
2. Meanwhile put the smoked Ricotta into a covered ovenproof dish and warm for a few minutes in a moderate oven at 350°F (180°C) Gas 4.
3. Arrange half the ravioli squares on the bottom of four warmed soup plates. Place a ½ tablespoonful of smoked Ricotta in the centre of each square and lay another pasta square on top. Grate black pepper over the pasta.
4. Heat the butter in a frying pan. As it heats, grate the nutmeg into it. As the butter browns take it off the heat. When the colour reaches a rich dark brown, pour in the lemon juice and spoon over the pasta.

ravioli paste as in the previous recipe
4 oz (100 g) smoked Ricotta
salt and freshly grated black pepper
8 oz (225 g) unsalted butter
½ fresh nutmeg
juice of 1 lemon

FRESH PASTA WITH SHELLFISH

Fish loves pasta. A twirl of fettucine with steamed lobster or sole is much more in harmony than potatoes of any sort. This recipe makes use of that affinity to produce a dish from the less expensive, though more fiddly, shellfish like cockles. If you have grander beasts to add, like langoustine or clams, so much the better. The key to the flavour is the molluscs, and sauce made without them won't taste as good.

The pasta

1. Sieve the flour with a good pinch of salt, then add the egg.
2. In a liquidiser blend the fresh herbs with the 2 tablespoons olive oil. Add this to the flour and egg mix and then beat well.

Belgian endive and goat's cheese pizza.

Charcoal grilled vegetables.

*Ragoût of wild mushrooms and baby vegetables. Photographed in the woods behind Gidleigh Park
with shaggy inkcaps growing out of the leaf mould.*

Open ravioli with chicken liver, lemon and garlic.

North sea fish soup photographed amongst the lobster pots in Brixham harbour at 6.30 in the morning.
Not necessarily the ideal time to eat it.

Sea bass with chinese spices. In the background is the North Teign river which rushes past the hotel.

Scallops with lentil and coriander sauce.

Gressingham duck with garlic and shallot confit and Sauternes sauce.

Serves 4

Pasta
4 oz (100 g) plain flour
salt
1 medium egg
1 tablespoon chopped, mixed
   fresh herbs, to include
   oregano and flat-leafed
   parsley
2 tablespoons olive oil

Shellfish sauce
8 oz (225 g) cockles
1 lb (450 g) mussels
8 oz (225 g) whole prawns
4 shallots, peeled
2 garlic cloves, peeled
olive oil
10 fl oz (300 ml) dry white cider
2 tablespoons tomato passata,
   or 2 whole ripe tomatoes
2 tablespoons double cream

The amount of oil you will need to use in making the dough may well vary according to the type of flour and the size of the egg you have used. Don't be afraid to add a little more oil if the mixture looks as if it needs it.
3.   Turn the dough out on to a floured board and knead well until it is a smooth elastic consistency.
4.   Cover the dough with a dampened cloth and allow to rest and relax for at least an hour in the refrigerator.
5.   Roll out the dough on a well floured surface until ⅛ in (3 mm) thick. Dust the dough with flour or fine semolina if it becomes difficult to work.
6.   Trim the sides and cut into ribbon shapes. If you have a pasta-rolling machine this will simplify matters considerably.

The shellfish sauce

7.   Carefully clean the cockles and mussels. The cockles will only need washing in clean water but mussels can be a real nuisance. Wash them through several changes of cold water, scrape off any barnacles or mud that may be attached to the shells, and yank out any beard there may be. The prawns will need shelling, and remember to keep the heads and shells for the sauce.
8.   Chop the shallots and garlic. Sweat them in a few drops of olive oil and then add the dry white cider.
9.   As soon as this boils add the cockles, mussels and prawn heads and shells. Put a tight-fitting lid on the saucepan, and cook for a couple of minutes. The mussels will have opened but should still be soft. Pick the cockles and mussels from their shells.
10.   Strain off the stock you have made into a clean saucepan, then re-boil it and whisk in the tomato passata or finely chopped tomato and the cream.
11.   Let this reduce until you have about 10 fl oz (300 ml) of sauce base. Whisk in 2 tablespoons of the olive oil so that it is incorporated in the sauce.

To complete

12.   Drop the pasta into a large saucepan of boiling salted water. As soon as it re-boils, drain the pasta in a colander. Try to remove as much water as possible. As you are shaking the pasta add a few drops more of olive oil so that the pasta doesn't stick together too much.
13.   Warm the sauce through with the shellfish.
14.   Add a little sauce to the pasta so that it sticks together, and then twirl it round a fork. Place one forkful in each of the four soup bowls and pour the shellfish sauce around it.

RED WINE RISOTTO

Risotto is made with Arborio rice, an Italian variety with rugby-football-shaped grains. It is more glutinous than long-grain Patna-type rices, but retains its texture better than mushy pudding rice.

Risotto suffers if overcooked, and is best with just a touch of resistance in the grains. This red wine risotto should be made with decent full-bodied wine. A *vino nobile* from Montepulciano or other good Italian wine will sound authentic and taste good, but a drinkable Cabernet Sauvignon from Chile will also suit.

A word on wine in cookery. Never buy anything called or advertised as cooking wine. They are uniformly drab, frequently smell awful and will spoil the food. Wine which is not drinkable is best poured down the sink.

In this dish, the wine is a major feature so use plenty. Normally I find that too much wine in a dish interferes with the flavours of the meat or fish and there is a danger that, after all your careful stock-making and hints of this and that, all your dishes may taste only of cheap wine. With a red wine risotto you may be generous.

The chicken stock

1.   Fry the chicken winglets and garlic in the oil until brown. Pour on 2 pints (1.2 litres) water and bring to the boil. Simmer for half an hour, until reduced by half, then add the marjoram or oregano and turn off the heat.
2.   After 10 minutes you may decant the stock either directly into the risotto or else into a clean container.

The risotto

3.   Heat the olive oil in a medium-sized saucepan, and sweat the onion for 3 minutes. Add the rice and continue to cook for a further 3 minutes without colouring. Season with salt and pepper, then pour on the red wine.
4.   Let the wine reduce completely and then add 10 fl oz (300 ml) of the stock. Bring this to the boil, stirring occasionally. Take the pan off the heat and leave the rice to absorb all the stock.

You may do all this in advance if you wish. A stainless steel saucepan will keep the purple colour of the wine, so use one if you can.

To complete

5.   Pour on the remaining stock. Bring to the boil and simmer until the stock is absorbed.
6.   Divide the risotto between heated plates. Serve with grated Parmesan and a thread of olive oil.

Serves 4

8 oz (225 g) Arborio rice
1 tablespoon olive oil
1 medium onion, peeled and
    chopped
salt and freshly ground black
    pepper
10 fl oz (300 ml) good red wine

Chicken stock (1 pint/600 ml)
8 oz (225 g) chicken winglets
1 garlic clove, peeled
1 tablespoon groundnut oil
1 sprig fresh marjoram or
    oregano

To complete
1 oz (25 g) Parmesan cheese,
    grated
extra virgin olive oil

Saffron Risotto with Steamed Vegetables

This is the traditional Milanese risotto. The vegetable garnish can be varied according to season; those here belong to early summer.

The vegetable stock

Serves 4

8 oz (225 g) Arborio rice
1 tablespoon olive oil
1 medium onion, peeled and chopped
salt and freshly ground black pepper
5 fl oz (150 ml) white wine
a pinch of saffron

Vegetable stock (1 pint/600 ml)
1 tablespoon groundnut oil
1 each of the following: small onion, garlic clove, carrot, celery stalk, aubergine, small potato

To complete
2 oz (50 g) unsalted butter
fresh Parmesan cheese
4 small carrots
4 courgettes
8 oz (225 g) French beans (about 12)
8 oz (225 g) mange-touts

Vegetable stock can be made any time and kept in the fridge or freezer.

1.   Heat the oil in a saucepan, then add the vegetables which should be peeled and sliced, as appropriate.
2.   As they begin to colour pour on 2 pints (1.2 litres) of water. Bring to the boil and then simmer for 40 minutes until reduced by half. Strain into a jug.

The risotto

3.   Heat the olive oil in a saucepan, and gently sweat the chopped onion for 3 minutes. Add the rice and continue to cook, without colouring, for a further 3 minutes. Season with salt and pepper and then pour on the white wine which will boil immediately.
4.   Let this wine reduce completely, about 5 minutes, and then add half the vegetable stock and the saffron, and re-boil. Take the pan off the heat and leave it until you are ready to complete the dish. As the rice cools it will continue to cook and absorb all the liquid.

To complete

5.   About 10 minutes before you are ready to eat, when you start to cook the vegetables, pour the rest of the stock on to the rice. Bring back to the boil, and add butter and 1 oz (25 g) grated Parmesan. Simmer on, and the risotto will be perfectly cooked when the stock has been absorbed.
6.   Put the prepared vegetables into the steamer in the order of time they take to cook – carrots, courgettes, then beans and lastly mange-touts. If you have no steamer and boil the vegetables, be sure the water is boiling before starting to cook.
7.   Spoon risotto on to each heated plate. Scatter the steamed vegetables on top, and decorate with a few shavings of fresh Parmesan.

Belgian Endive and Goat's Cheese Pizza

A very thin base with spicy topping is the aim here for a hot starter or, at most, a light lunch with salad.

The fresh, in fresh goat's cheese, refers to the manufacture method rather than how recently it was purchased. Cabri or English Perroche are good examples.

White flour may be replaced in part with wholemeal or even rye, but at a cost to the pizza's lightness. The only other tip I can offer is to leave the edges of the pizza a fraction thicker so that the topping all stays put.

The pizza bases

1.   Dissolve the yeast in the tepid milk. Mix thoroughly and leave to stand in a warm place for 15 minutes until it becomes frothy.
2.   Add ½ teaspoon salt, the olive oil and then the flour. You should have a soft, slightly sticky, yet workable dough.
3.   Knead it for about 5 minutes then place in a large oiled bowl, cover with cling film and leave in a warm place to rise until doubled in volume. This should take between 30 minutes and 1 hour, but depends on room temperature.
4.   Split the dough into four balls and then roll out on a floured surface to ⅛ in (3 mm). You may pull the dough into shape with your fingers if it helps as it is quite elastic. Cover loosely with cling film while you make the topping.
5.   Preheat the oven to 475°F (240°C) Gas 9. Put a thick baking sheet or four appropriately sized, handleless metal pans into the oven to preheat for 15 minutes.

The topping

6.   Acidulate a saucepan of water with the lemon juice and then boil the endives for 10 minutes. Lift them out and pat them dry with kitchen paper. Cut each endive in half lengthwise and remove the first ¼ in (6 mm) of hard base.
7.   Fry the onion and garlic in 2 tablespoons of the olive oil until soft, about 3 or 4 minutes. Add the tomato and season with salt and pepper. Turn the tomato in the oil, garlic and onion for 2 minutes so that it starts to melt but still has a fresh smell. Remove from the heat.

To complete

8.   Brush the pizza bases with olive oil. Spread on the onion and tomato mix. Place a half endive and goat cheese, also split in half, on each base.
9.   Take the hot baking tray or pans out of the oven. Brush pans and pizzas with olive oil and bake for 10 minutes. Serve immediately.

Serves 4

Pizza bases
¼ oz (7.5 g) fresh yeast
5 fl oz (150 ml) milk
salt
1 tablespoon olive oil
8 oz (225 g) strong plain white
   flour

Topping
juice of ½ lemon
2 Belgian endives (chicory)
1 onion, peeled and finely
   sliced
2 garlic cloves, peeled and
   crushed
olive oil
3 plum tomatoes, skinned, de-
   seeded and chopped
freshly ground black pepper
4 small fresh goat's cheeses

Welsh Rarebit

Welsh rarebit used to be served regularly as a savoury course at the very end of a meal. It is better as a snack with aperitifs before the start of a meal, or as a light lunch.

This recipe produces a warming and savoury Welsh rarebit. I don't like it too hot and peppery, and have never subscribed to the vindaloo school of thought which equates one's capacity for very hot food with one's virility.

Serves 4

½ oz (15 g) butter
1 teaspoon plain flour
1 fl oz (25 ml) milk
1 tablespoon Dijon mustard
8 oz (225 g) mature Cheddar cheese, grated
2 fl oz (50 ml) stout
black pepper
1 teaspoon Worcestershire sauce
1 medium egg
4 slices of the bread you prefer

1. Melt the butter in a small saucepan. Add the flour and stir over a low heat to form a little roux. When the roux comes cleanly away from the bottom of the pan it is cooked.
2. Add the drop of milk and stir until combined, and it too comes cleanly away from the pan surface.
3. Add the mustard, cheese, beer and pepper. Stir with a wooden spoon over the same low heat until it is all combined. Let the mixture come to the boil which it does with all the grace of a hot mud spring.
4. Remove the pan from the heat. Add the Worcestershire sauce and egg. Stir the latter in quickly or it will cook before being incorporated.
5. Allow this mixture to cool.
6. Toast the bread lightly on both sides. Spread the mixture thickly on top and return to the grill to glaze.

Tunafish and Spring Onion Sandwich

Makes 2 sandwiches

1 × 7 oz (200 g) tin tuna
2 tablespoons mayonnaise (see page 123)
4 spring onions, cleaned and thinly sliced
a pinch of salt and plenty of freshly ground black pepper
4 slices granary bread

Tinned tuna is a really versatile store-cupboard item. Don't automatically sneer at tinned or even frozen products. Hawaiian yellowfin tuna may be one of the world's great fish to eat fresh, but I have no easy access to it. Nor would it suit my sandwich as well as tinned supermarket bonito. More important to worry about is the bread. Flabby white sliced will not do.

1. Turn the tuna out into a bowl.
2. Add the mayonnaise, spring onion, salt and pepper. Mix together with a fork.
3. Spread the tuna mixture thickly on two slices of the bread (you won't need butter). Top with the other slices to make your sandwich.

GRILLED MOZZARELLA, MARJORAM AND LATE SUMMER TOMATO SANDWICH

Fresh goat's cheese, perhaps Cabri or Perroche, would also taste good in this sandwich.

Makes 2 sandwiches

1 × 6 oz (175 g) fresh Mozzarella cheese
1 tablespoon double cream
1 small sprig fresh marjoram
4 slices crusty white bread
1 tablespoon olive oil
2 large tomatoes, skinned
freshly ground black pepper

1. Drain the cheese, then mash it and the cream together in a bowl with a fork.
2. Pick the marjoram leaves into the cheese.
3. Brush the bread slices on one side with olive oil and then lightly toast on both sides under a grill.
4. Spread the cheese and herb filling over the oiled side of the toast. Slice tomatoes on top and then grind plenty of black pepper over the lot.
5. Return the toast to the grill for 1 minute to heat through the filling. Combine the toasts to make the sandwiches.

3

FISH AND SHELLFISH

A lot of chefs will tell you that fish is what they like to cook most, often implying some great skill. Fish is quite easy to cook, though, and the difficulty is in tracking down really good raw materials. There's more variety in fish than meat, with a range of textures and flavours from those with fragile flesh and delicate flavour like sole and whiting to coarse, almost meaty fish like porbeagle shark. Obviously they're all good for different things: red mullet will take robust flavourings like red peppers or powerful olive oil dressings which would overpower a fish like Dover sole. Generally, with fish, you should work with a light hand. You are dealing with quite delicate flavours on the whole, and an extravagant use of any powerful herb like fennel or thyme will dominate the dish.

There is no best method of cooking fish. They're all good for most fish. My only observation is that as a method, steaming is neglected and that steamed fish partners butter sauces to perfection. I would only poach rather than steam fish when I needed the stock. Fish cooks quite quickly, and is easy to overcook, making it drier and duller. Fish like salmon grill particularly well, and are better slightly underdone. Roasting needs to be done in a very hot oven, sealing the flesh so that it will keep in the moisture and juices. The technique of deep-frying fish is the same as deep-frying anything else; the quality of oil and temperature of frying are crucial. Shallow-frying is straightforward enough as well. Use an oil like groundnut, and add only a few drops of oils such as olive or sesame if those are the flavours you require. Most of all, remember to heat the pan well before you start.

Sea fish

Sea fish are the last properly free-range food, and they are better fresh than frozen. This may seem pompously self-evident but it isn't. Quite a few things freeze well, fresh herb purées and stock, for instance. It is important to remember the opposite of fresh is stale and not frozen, but in this case it shouldn't be necessary. Most of our fish comes from the North Atlantic, and we should not accept frozen just to make life easier for those who sell it.

We are very lucky to be surrounded by those really great fishing grounds of the North Atlantic. The parts of the globe which are coloured blue may all be sea or water but are not all full of fish that are good to eat. Fishermen tend to hunt for a specific quarry and they take great skill to track their likely whereabouts. The different species of fish and shellfish live in different parts, determined by factors like water temperature, salinity and water depth, the availability of food. The warm currents of the Gulf Stream make great diversity possible. It is a fascinating subject, and I suggest you read Alan Davidson's *North Atlantic Seafood* if you want to find out, for instance, why there should be more sea bass in the summer or why some species migrate huge distances to spawn or feed.

There are general categories that sea fish fall into like the cod family, flat fish, the herring family, molluscs and crustaceans. You are almost always better off to approach fish purchase with flexibility within one of these groups. You don't have to be Escoffier to work out that good turbot is better than tired halibut and vice versa. Success with fish all comes down ultimately to purchasing skill. Fish does not improve with age. People have told me that skate is better a few days after landing, and I've heard the same for one or two other fish. I have never found this. What I do find is that after a few days fish starts to look tired and boring, and will certainly taste the same.

Freshwater fish

I have never been a keen fisherman, and I have always pondered the sanity of those who sit in the cold and wet, stalking a prey of trout or bream. I'm delighted when they trap a good carp or trout, but have never been enormously taken by some of the bony creatures that people will sit up all night to catch.

The two kings of freshwater fish are salmon and sea trout. They are both really sea fish and better caught at the estuary than further upstream. Sea trout is probably my favourite fish, with a flavour that manages to be delicate without being insipid. I suppose I should mention farmed salmon and trout. Farmed salmon are quite adequate, but can never achieve the peaks of flavour of a wild fish. Farmed trout on the other hand are universally mediocre and the farmed versions of sea trout, carefully called salmon trout, are only large rainbows fed with some strange substance to colour the flesh pink. With salmon trout, as with all the other pleasures of life, you can't beat the real thing.

RED MULLET WITH GINGER, GARLIC AND TOMATO

Red mullet doesn't suit creamy sauces. It may be something connected with natural oils in the fish, but the prospects of this fish with cream or mushrooms doesn't excite me. This sauce reads as strong and dominant but, in fact, tastes gently spicy.

The fish

Serves 4

2 × 14 oz (400 g) red mullet
salt

Sauce
5 fl oz (150 ml) fish stock (or water and wine, see method)
8 plum tomatoes
1 tablespoon groundnut oil
2 oz (50 g) shallots, peeled and chopped
2 oz (50 g) knob ginger, peeled and very finely diced
4 garlic cloves, peeled and chopped
1 small chilli, chopped
2 oz (50 g) butter
1 sprig fresh coriander, chopped
2 spring onions, trimmed and chopped

To complete
½ lemon

1.   The mullet needs filleting for this dish (see page 42). The two mullet should give four fat fillets. Score the skin with four or five shallow knife-strokes and season with salt.

The sauce

2.   If you don't have fish stock, wash the fish trimmings and bones under cold water, then put them in a saucepan with 10 fl oz (300 ml) cold water and a dash of white wine. Bring to the boil and then leave to cool. The liquor you strain off will be an acceptable substitute for stock in this instance.
3.   You need well-flavoured, firm tomatoes such as Italian plum or beefsteak tomatoes. Skin them by dropping into boiling water for a few seconds and then peeling. Cut them into quarters, scoop out and discard the seeds and then cut into ¼ in (6 mm) squares.
4.   Warm the groundnut oil in a saucepan and add the shallots, ginger, garlic and chilli. Cook them for 2 minutes without colouring then add the diced tomato and fish stock. Bring to the boil and simmer for 2 minutes. Stir in the butter, chopped coriander and spring onion. Don't forget a pinch of salt.

To complete

5.   Turn the fish fillets over on a lightly oiled plate then grill under a high heat with the skin side towards the flame until just cooked. Mullet cooks quite quickly so this should only take 5 minutes under a hot grill.
6.   Pour the sauce on to warmed plates. Squeeze the lemon on to the fish, place the fish on top of the sauce, and serve immediately.

STEAMED RED MULLET WITH BITTER SALADS AND OLIVE OIL DRESSING

This mullet dish is in the tradition of many Mediterranean fish dishes which are cooked and served with olive oil. *Escabeche* comes to mind. Unless the mullet are tiny I prefer to fillet them. The bones are messy on the plate with a salad, and unless you are an accomplished eater they are inclined to make the meal more of a challenge than a pleasure. The mullet flesh cooks quickly, much quicker than sea bass for instance. You may grill the fish if you prefer, but if you do, you must just grill through the skin side only. This will make the skin edible and the flesh still juicy. If you are going to serve the mullet warm it is better steamed. An oil-based dressing over grilled fish would give an oily taste, whereas steamed fish will have a cleaner feel that welcomes the oil dressing in the same way that butter sauces always go better with steamed or poached fish.

The addition of a little parsley pesto sauce adds an extra dimension to the dish, though it isn't essential.

Serves 4 as a starter

2 × 8 oz (225 g) red mullet
a selection of salad leaves:
  curly endive, lollo rosso,
  dandelion leaves and batavia
1 lemon
salt and freshly ground pepper
4 tomatoes, skinned, de-seeded
  and diced

Dressing
1 teaspoon coriander seeds,
  crushed
1 garlic clove, peeled
2 sprigs thyme
5 fl oz (150 ml) extra virgin olive
  oil

Flat parsley pesto
1 oz (25 g) pine kernels
1 fl oz (25 ml) olive oil
1 oz (25 g) flat leaf parsley,
  chopped
1 garlic clove, peeled
1 fl oz (25 ml) fish stock (see
  page 121) or white wine

The mullet

1.   Scale the fish by scraping them from tail to head at an acute angle with a sharp knife. This is a messy process and the scales will fly everywhere if you are not careful. Try not to work next to all your best salad things.
2.   There is a sharp dorsal fin along the ridge of the backbone. Cut carefully along this line until you come to the backbone. Keep your knife pointed slightly inwards. This way if your hand slips you'll cut fish and not finger. Also, you should find that there is a line of bone which will prevent your knife cutting across into the opposite side. The process is easier than it sounds and you shouldn't be daunted by it. After all it is only the common sense of removing flesh from bone that you are about.
3.   Wash the fillets of fish and pat dry immediately.
4.   If you run your finger along the centre of each fillet from top to bottom you will find there is a series of small bones. If these worry you they are easily removed with a pair of tweezers.

The salad leaves

5.   Thoroughly wash the salad leaves. Make sure that the water is cold so that the salad will be crisp. It is best if you run a basin full of cold water and dunk your leaves in it. This way any grit that there may be in there will loosen and sink to the bottom.

6. Drying salad leaves thoroughly is as important as washing. Shake each leaf thoroughly. Too much water will dilute the dressing and make the leaves flabby.

The dressing

7. Put the crushed coriander seeds, whole garlic and the sprigs of thyme into the olive oil with some peel from the lemon, and warm through gently. Allow it to cool.

To complete

8. Season your salad leaves with salt and pepper and then arrange in a circle along the outside of each individual plate.
9. Liquidise the pesto ingredients, with a squeeze of lemon juice, to produce a pale green, creamy sauce.
10. Steam the mullet until it is just cooked, about 5 minutes for an 8 oz (225 g) mullet. If larger, cook longer; it is done when the flesh starts to form flakes. (If you have no steamer or double saucepan, cook the fish in a shallow pan with only 2 or 3 tablespoonfuls of stock or wine and a tight-fitting lid to cover the pan. When the liquid evaporates it will produce steam and cook the fish very quickly.)
11. Place a spoonful of the pesto sauce in the centre of each plate. Squeeze a few drops of lemon juice over the fish fillets, then lift them carefully on to the pesto sauce.
12. Spoon the tomato dice on to the fish fillets, and spoon the dressing over the fish and salads.

NORTH SEA FISH SOUP

All my favourite aspects of cookery find their way into this dish. There is no waste: fish skin, bones, and prawn shells all impart something to the flavour of the dish. There is slow cooking and careful extraction of tastes from the less appealing parts coupled with the immediacy and freshness of fish just cooked at the last moment.

The ingredients in the recipe are a guideline only, and it is the technique which produces the dish. The soup is quick to make and the preparation work isn't hard.

It is a more interesting dish if you use small amounts of four or five different fishes. But if you are embarrassed to make your fishmonger work for his living by weighing out several things in small amounts, it will work with only two types, so long as they are of different textures like scallops and halibut.

Bear in mind, too, that some fish cook more quickly than others. You will need to cut sea bass into smaller pieces than scallops for instance, or else put it into the stock a few moments earlier so that both will be cooked at the same time.

Use a large spoon for tasting. Soup isn't sauce, and the seasoning and cream content are different. What tastes fine in a teaspoon isn't necessarily good by the bowlful.

The stock

1.   Wash the bones and trimmings from the fish, along with the red scallop corals, prawn shells and bodies, under cold running water. Wash the stalks from the parsley too.
2.   In a medium saucepan turn these over with a knob of the butter until they start to smell cooked. Add the wine and 1½ pints (900 ml) of cold water. Bring this to the boil and then simmer for 10 minutes. The water should just cover the bones and fish scraps: if it doesn't you are using the wrong size of pan.
3.   Strain this stock into a clean saucepan. You should have over a pint (600 ml) of well-flavoured liquid.

The soup

4.   Skin the tomatoes by dropping them for a few seconds in boiling water and then peeling them. Cut them in half and then scoop out and discard the seeds from the middle. Dice the tomato flesh.
5.   Wash the parsley leaves in plenty of cold water, then drain well and chop. Parsley often contains quite a bit of grit and sand which will drop to the bottom of the sink if the parsley is actually suspended in water.

Serves 4

3 oz (75 g) sea bass fillet
3 oz (75 g) hake fillet
3 oz (75 g) haddock fillet
4 scallops
3 oz (75 g) whole prawns
1 small bunch parsley
2 oz (50 g) unsalted butter
2½ fl oz (65 ml) dry white wine
2 tomatoes
1 slice good white bread
2 shallots
juice of 1 lemon
salt and freshly ground black
   pepper

To complete
2 egg yolks
2 tablespoons double cream

6.   Cut the bread into ¼ in (6 mm) cubes. Fry them until a golden brown colour in the foaming butter. Strain off the butter and pat the croûtons dry with kitchen paper.

7.   Peel and chop the shallots. Add these to the stock and bring this back to the boil.

8.   Cut each piece of fish, and each scallop, into four pieces, and turn them briefly in lemon juice. Season them with salt and pepper and then add them to the stock, remembering to add them in order of which fish takes longest to cook – sea bass first, then hake, then haddock, and lastly the scallops. the whole process shouldn't take more than 2 minutes, and the scallops no more than about 30 seconds. Remember that they will continue to 'cook' from now until eaten.

To complete

9.   As soon as the soup approaches boiling point remove the pan from the heat. In a small bowl whisk together the egg yolks and cream. Add a little of the soup to this mixture, whisking as you do so. Pour the egg-cream liaison back into the soup and stir it carefully so as not to break up the pieces of fish. Now taste a spoonful of the soup. It will certainly need salt and quite possibly a few more drops of lemon juice.

This soup should taste like its ingredients and not be dominated by any strong herb or vegetable. It's important, though, to get the seasoning right. If you forget salt the soup will taste bland. It's worth spending time tasting in the final stages.

Remember, too, that once you have added the egg-cream liaison you should not re-boil the soup or it will curdle. The sooner you eat this soup once you have made it the better it will taste.

10.   Put the croûtons, parsley, prawns and tomato in a warm terrine. Pour on the soup and serve it straightaway.

SEA BASS WITH CHINESE SPICES

My favourite Chinese restaurant in the sixties was closed down by the health inspector. I never suffered a bad stomach after eating there, but the chef had taken to keeping live poultry in the kitchen, which is against the rules.

The sort of Chinese restaurant I like features food which many find bizarre. You probably don't normally tuck into chicken feet and jellyfish, but you shouldn't be prejudiced against trying these interesting flavours and textures.

The one unifying feature in Chinese restaurants is the consistent rudeness of the waiters, but I discovered the reason for this when I worked in Soho. Most of these chaps gamble their money at Mah Jong or on horses. How much tip you leave is therefore considerably less important than whether luck smiles on them. It has now become part of the treat to be served with curled lip and averted eye, and I would miss it if I weren't. There is more than one sort of hospitality, and in Chinese restaurants, the food's the thing.

There are plenty of good Oriental supermarkets in larger cities, with large choice of noodles, specialist cooking equipment and Chinese spices, including five-spice powder, a mixture of star anise, anise pepper, fennel seed, cassia and cloves. (And if you find out why disgusting bright red food colouring is so much prized in Cantonese cooking I would be obliged if you would let me know.)

The flavour of sea bass marries well with Chinese spices and treatment. A dish without butter or cream will allow you to eat a creamy starter or dessert, and yet finish the meal not feeling queasy with cholesterol.

The vegetable garnish

1. Peel the carrot; trim the leek; halve and de-seed the red pepper; trim the courgette. Keep all the trimmings for the sauce.
2. With a potato peeler shave the carrot and then the courgette into thin slices. Cut into thin strips.
3. Cut the leek into manageable lengths then slice into long, thin strips. Wash them carefully and pat dry.
4. Slice the red pepper as thinly as you can and mix it together with the other strips of vegetables.

The fish

I prefer to use fillets from larger fish rather than several small fish. The dish is like *pot au feu* and you should drink the cooking liquors as well as eat the fish. This is much easier if you have no head or bones to contend with.

Serves 4

1 × 2 lb (900 g) sea bass

Sauce
fish bones
trimmings from all the
   vegetables
1 knob fresh ginger, peeled and
   crushed
2 garlic cloves, peeled
1 tablespoon soy sauce,
   preferably Japanese
1 pinch five-spice powder
6 spring onions, trimmed and
   chopped

Vegetable garnish
1 carrot
1 leek
1 red pepper
1 courgette

5. Carefully scale the fish with a sharp knife moving from the tail towards the head.
6. Use the same sharp knife to remove the fillets from the fish following the line of the spine from head to tail.

The sauce

7. Cut the fish bones into 2 in (5 cm) pieces. Mix with the trimmings from the vegetables, and add the ginger and garlic. Pour on a pint (600 ml) of water and bring to the boil. Allow to simmer for 20 minutes.
8. Strain the stock into a new saucepan. Add the soy sauce and boil to reduce by about a third.

To complete

9. Preheat the oven to 400°F (200°C) Gas 6.
10. Place the fillets of fish in a casserole or roasting tray with the skin side upmost, and pour your soy-flavoured stock over them.
11. Bake the fish in the oven for about 10 minutes until just cooked.
12. Carefully lift out the fillets, keep warm, and pour the sauce into a saucepan. Re-boil and cook the garnish vegetables in this liquor, only a minute or so if you have cut them really thinly.
13. Place the fish fillets on individual plates, and arrange the vegetables in a little bundle on top of each. Finish the sauce with a pinch of five-spice powder and the chopped spring onion, then pour this around the fish.

GRILLED SEA TROUT WITH WATERCRESS AND MOREL MUSHROOMS

Most fish have individual nuances of flavour rather than the powerful tastes of beef or game. When you are deciding whether to steam, poach or grill, consider whether the sauce or accompaniment will be too much for the fish. A sauce should either derive from the fish through its stock, or else highlight its flavour by providing a contrast. Grilling gives you a more concentrated taste that eats well with a robust flavoured sauce or vegetables which might have dominated a poached fish dish.

Salmon or sea trout grills very well. Its flavour is best if it is cooked with a fierce heat so that the skin becomes quite dark and crisp. If you fillet the fish, as I do, then cook it through the skin, not turning the flesh side towards the heat. This way the fish stays moist and the skin becomes crisp and delicious to eat. The same is true for salmon and red mullet.

This dish uses watercress and morel mushrooms to provide a contrast of flavour. Be careful not to use too much watercress, for although it gives a pretty green colour and is delicious in moderation, used in any quantity it would dominate the dish. If you cannot obtain morel mushrooms then leave them out rather than substitute with button mushrooms. If you cannot get crème fraîche then use double cream and finish the sauce with a few drops of lemon juice.

The fish

Serves 4

1. Scale the fish. Use a sharp knife and work from tail to head. Clean up the mess.
2. If you are going to fillet the trout then do so now, remembering to cut along the backbone. With a pair of tweezers pull out the line of small bones that run along the centre of each fillet.
3. Brush the fillets with a little groundnut oil.

1 × 2½ lb (1.1 kg) sea trout
groundnut oil
coarse sea salt
lemon juice

Sauce
1 oz (25 g) dried morel
   mushrooms
fish bones
2 fl oz (50 ml) dry vermouth
2 oz (50 g) shallots, peeled and
   finely chopped
4 fl oz (120 ml) dry white wine
4 new potatoes
4 fl oz (120 ml) crème fraîche (or
   cream and lemon juice)
4 oz (100 g) unsalted butter
1 small bunch watercress

The sauce

4. Soak the mushrooms in water for an hour or two. Cut them in half lengthways and wash them carefully as they often have tiny stones and grit in the middle. Boil them in a little water for a few seconds, drain and then allow them to cool.
5. If you have filleted the sea trout then wash the bones and cut them into 1 in (2.5 cm) lengths. Infuse them with the vermouth, chopped shallot and

10 fl oz (300 ml) water by bringing to the boil and allowing to cool. Strain off the liquid.

6. Add the white wine to this liquid and bring to the boil. Let it simmer until it has reduced by half.

7. Scrub and then dice the potatoes, and add to the stock. Whisk in the crème fraîche and bring to the boil again, by which time the potato dice will be cooked.

8. Whisk in the unsalted butter, piece by piece, incorporating it into the sauce. This should have the effect of thickening it slightly.

9. Carefully wash and pat dry the watercress. Chop it roughly and then add it to the sauce. Test for salt and pepper. If you have used double cream instead of crème fraîche, now is the time to add a few drops of lemon juice. Keep warm.

To complete

10. Preheat the grill so that you will seal the sea trout as soon as you start cooking it.

11. Salt the skin side of the fish with coarse sea salt. Grill it through the skin until it is just cooked or even a little under-cooked, about 10 minutes for a ¾ in (2 cm) thick sea trout fillet.

12. Squeeze a few drops of lemon on to the fish and serve on individual warmed plates on top of the sauce.

Understanding by touch if the fish is cooked gets easier with experience. Fish cooked on the bone just won't be filleted unless it is properly cooked, but fish cooked in fillets needs to be pressed or squeezed slightly. What you are feeling for is a springy, slightly rubbery reaction as if there were something tough or hard inside. This means it isn't cooked and except with fish like salmon you will need a few moments more.

MONKFISH WITH MUSTARD AND CUCUMBER SAUCE

Were there monkfish before 1975? We all know the horse took several million years to evolve, but under the influence of Messrs Troisgros, Chapel and Blanc, the *lotte* became established in our gastronomic consciousness in no time at all.

Before that its real claim to fame was as the Tom Keating of the piscine world, a supposed underhand catering substitute for scampi because of its knotty, dense texture. An erstwhile neighbour assured me that lobster in fancy restaurants is always 'that angler fish'. (In that distant age many otherwise sensible people were suspicious of restaurants: they thought that Chinese restaurants always served rabbit as chicken, and that sauces were a guise to mask inferior meat. This from the same people that cheerfully put green colouring, mint and vinegar on good lamb, and who wouldn't try food that had been 'mucked about'.)

Discovery, or at least respectability, came with the arrival of *La Nouvelle Cuisine*. Not only was the fish fashionable; it was cheaper than sole or sea bass. Restaurateurs couldn't ask for anything more, and it appeared on every menu. I don't think it can taste any different now than then, and I'm amazed that anyone could confuse it with scampi – it's much better.

The monkfish

1.   With a small sharp knife cut away the two fillets from the one central bone. Try to keep the knife pointed slightly inwards towards the bone so that if your hand slips you are cutting against the bone rather than damaging the fish fillet. Cut away the two 'cheeks' which are attached to the fillets, then carefully trim off the membrane and any discoloured patches.

If you are not going to use the fish immediately, put it in the refrigerator either wrapped in cling film if it is to be used within a few hours, or else lightly brushed with olive oil. Remember not to put the fish next to eggs, milk or anything else likely to taint.

2.   Just before you complete the dish, slice the fish into medallions no more than ¼ in (6 mm) thick.

The fish stock

3.   Cut the bone and all the fish trimmings into roughly 1 in (2.5 cm) pieces. Clean and cut the leek, shallot and parsley similarly. Grind a little black pepper over the pieces.

Serves 4

1 lb (450 g) monkfish flesh taken from the bone (see left)
olive oil
salt and freshly ground black pepper

Fish stock
fish bone and trimmings
1 medium leek
1 medium shallot
1 small bunch parsley

Sauce
1 cucumber, peeled
1 tablespoon Dijon mustard
1 fl oz (25 ml) dry sherry
2 fl oz (50 ml) double cream
1 oz (25 g) unsalted butter

To complete
½ lemon

4.   Warm a teaspoon of olive oil in a medium (say 2 pint/1.2 litre) saucepan, then sweat the fish bones and trimmings and vegetables until you can smell cooked fish rather than raw.

5.   Add all the peelings from the cucumber and 1 pint (600 ml) water. Bring this to the boil then turn down the heat and simmer for 20 minutes.

6.   Strain into a smaller saucepan and reduce by simmering until you have 5 fl oz (150 ml) left.

The sauce

7.   Cut the cucumber, as you prefer, either into thin slices or thin strips. Lightly salt and pepper them. Keep them to one side in a warm spot in the kitchen.

8.   Whisk the mustard and sherry into the fish stock and bring to the boil.

9.   Add the cream. Re-boil and then simmer for 5 minutes. Whisk in the butter, and take the sauce off the heat.

To complete

10.   Heat a dry pan until you sense it is about to start smoking. Place the thin slices of monkfish on to the hot surface of the pan and let them seal on each side. Dust with a fine spray of salt. They will cook in 2 or 3 minutes.

11.   Lift the slices of monkfish on to a piece of kitchen paper and squeeze lemon over them.

12.   Test the sauce to see whether it may need a little salt. Spoon the sauce on to warm plates.

13.   Lift the cucumber which will have shed some of its juices. Squeeze it lightly and place on to the sauce.

14.   Lay the monkfish on top, and serve immediately.

Carp Quenelles with Shrimps and Dill

Middle European countries eat a lot of freshwater fish like carp and sander. It makes sense when you look at the atlas – most do not have a lot of seaside.

I first came upon carp at the Gay Hussar, a Hungarian restaurant in Soho, when I worked there in the early seventies. There was a tank full of them in an otherwise cramped kitchen. They swam lazily about in spacious surrounds while we cooks could barely move without stabbing each other. The kitchen was peopled with Austrians and Hungarians, most of whom had fought on the wrong side in the last war. Old Paul, an Austrian, not only taught me how to make *knoedl* and dumplings but also marked out on the chopping block why his platoon lost almost every engagement on the Russian Front. Ferenc, a Hungarian, had greater skills. He could not only make wonderful strudel pastry, but could transform a small pot of goulash into a bottle of wine through a little astute bargaining with the wine merchant next door.

The carp were netted and killed as needed, and I was very squeamish about this at the time. We served them deep-fried in beer batter or roasted in great chunks like a Sunday joint. They were best of all, though, served as in this recipe.

Carp has more flavour and makes better quenelles than pike. Quenelles are not difficult to make but there are a few basic ground rules. More egg white makes for a lighter end product but you tend to lose flavour and end up with fishy meringue if you use too many. Two whites from size 4 eggs are a good compromise for this amount of quenelle mixture. Using a liquidiser will save you having to pass the entire mixture through a sieve, a very laborious process. Take care, though, that the mixture doesn't become too warm at any stage while you're beating or processing it, or the quenelles will become runny and not hold together. Lastly, this recipe uses shrimps to flavour the sauce and to balance the lightness of the quenelles. When you buy these they will be already cooked so don't cook them any more or they will dry out – just warm them through in the sauce at the end.

The stock

Ask for the bones of the carp and any other bones your fishmonger will give you, preferably from well-flavoured white fish, like sole or turbot. When you are peeling your shrimps keep all your peelings together in a bowl to flavour the stock. Similarly, when you are picking the dill away from the stalks, keep the stalks to one side.

Serves 4

10 oz (275 g) carp fillet
4 oz (100 g) pink shrimps
1 small bunch dill
2 egg whites
10 fl oz (300 ml) double cream
salt and freshly ground pepper

Stock
1 small leek
5 fl oz (150 ml) dry vermouth

To complete
4 oz (100 g) unsalted butter
5 fl oz (150 ml) crème fraîche

1.   Thinly slice the leek. Wash it carefully and then put it into a saucepan with the fish bones, shrimp peelings and dill stalks. Add about a pint (600 ml) of water and the vermouth.
2.   Bring this to a gentle simmer for about 10 minutes. Turn off the heat and then allow it to cool.
3.   Sieve the stock into a clean saucepan ready to cook your quenelles.

The carp quenelles

4.   Cut the carp flesh into manageable pieces and then chop in a food processor.
5.   Add the egg whites one by one.
6.   Transfer this mixture into a liquidiser with the cream, and add salt and pepper. The mixture will probably take about a teaspoon of salt. Process until this mixture is completely smooth.
7.   With two spoons, form eight equal-sized quenelles and put them in the fish stock, which should be simmering gently.
8.   Allow the quenelles to poach gently for about 5 minutes and then with a slotted spoon turn them over to cook for another 5 minutes.

The texture and shape of the quenelles depends first on your keeping the mixture cool while you are making it, and second, on poaching properly. If the mixture gets too warm, they will fall apart. If they are boiled fiercely they will puff up like soufflés. If you eat them immediately this is fine, and they will be very light, but after a minute they will sink back looking cracked and deflated. While poaching, keep the stock simmering but do not let it get to a rolling boil. The quenelles should have a pronounced but delicate fish flavour.

To complete

9.   With a slotted spoon remove the quenelles from the stock and drain them on kitchen paper, keeping warm.
10.   Rapidly boil the stock until it reduces by half.
11.   Whisk in the unsalted butter piece by piece, until it thickens the sauce.
12.   Whisk in the crème fraîche, snipped dill and the shrimps. Taste the sauce, it will need a little bit of salt.
13.   Place the quenelles on warmed plates and spoon the sauce on top.

SCALLOPS WITH LENTIL AND CORIANDER SAUCE

Gidleigh Park's menu uses a lot of expensive ingredients like caviar and foie gras, and I want this to be balanced by dishes which are more mundane – this doesn't mean boring and drab, but 'earthy'. The lentil sauce for the purée should be spicy and aromatic, and the cream and butter will counter any fierce or dominant taste and give the base a smooth texture. The freshness and flavour of the coriander leaves contrasts with the earthy character of the lentil purée, yet they blend together extremely well. Fresh coriander is essential for its aroma – seeds or the dried herb don't give the same effect.

This is just about my current favourite dish, but I wouldn't want you to think that the recipe arrived whole and complete like a tablet from Mount Sinai. The dish began as an unsuccessful experiment with lobster and a lightly curried lentil purée, progressed through lobster and scallop with lentil purée, and then became scallops with lentil purée, lemon and coriander leaves, a definite improvement. The purée developed into a sauce base with butter and cream, and the fresh coriander, at one point just one of many small ingredients, was elevated to co-star status. The final dish tastes right to me, and I offer my regrets to anyone who ate it during its progress to that stage.

Take special care buying molluscs, especially in summer. Everyone is concerned about oysters and avoids them in months without Rs. The worst stomach ache I ever experienced came from scallops. They had warned me by smelling like a drain, and had I taken note, I would have spent less time over one.

The sauce

The base for this can be made up to 12 hours in advance.

1. Soak the lentils for at least 4 hours, but preferably overnight, with occasional water changes, then parboil in salt water until tender, usually about 5 minutes. Drain.
2. Fry the onion, garlic and ginger in some of the oil until golden.
3. Add the crushed cardamom and allow to cook off the heat for a few seconds, then add tomatoes and two-thirds of the cooked lentils.
4. Cut the corals from the scallops and clean (see opposite).
5. Bring the chicken stock to the boil, add the corals, cook for 5 or 10 minutes, and sieve the coral stock on to the lentil mixture. Throw away the corals.
6. Simmer for 10 minutes, then purée in a liquidiser.

Serves 4

16 large, very fresh scallops
sesame or groundnut oil

Sauce
2 oz (50 g) brown lentils
salt
½ onion, peeled and chopped
1 large garlic clove, peeled and crushed
1 knob fresh ginger, peeled and crushed
1 teaspoon cardamom seeds, crushed
2 large, ripe tomatoes, skinned, or 2 tablespoons tomato passata
10 fl oz (300 ml) chicken stock

To complete
2 oz (50 g) unsalted butter
1 tablespoon crème fraîche or soured cream
juice of ½ lemon
1 small bunch fresh coriander, chopped

The scallops

These must be very fresh. They should be washed at the last moment (no more than 20 minutes before cooking), and shouldn't be in contact with water any longer than necessary to clean off any grit or sand. Never use frozen scallops for this dish, nor any that have been soaked in water (a common fishmonger's practice to make them swell). Waterlogged scallops will always stick to the pan as they cook, then shrivel and toughen as the water bubbles out.

7. Clean the scallops, then cut horizontally into three or four slices and brush with oil. Use an oil which will enhance the flavour of the dish, like sesame or groundnut, and avoid highly flavoured oils like olive. You need only the finest coating of oil if the pan is hot enough.

To complete

8. Reheat lentil purée in a clean pan, whisking in butter, cream and lemon juice. Check salt.
9. Add the coriander leaves and remaining whole warm lentils to the sauce. Spoon the sauce on to plates.
10. Cook the lightly oiled scallop slices in a very hot dry frying pan for a few seconds on each side, and lay them on the sauce.

You are aiming for a golden, caramelised outside with a soft and barely cooked inside. It's important to have your frying pan really hot to get the dish right – if the scallops boil or steam they will lose the concentrated flavour needed to balance the sauce.

SCALLOPS WITH CARAMELISED ENDIVES

This dish has no sauce other than the drops of caramel which coat the endive. Nor does it need one. Its effect relies on the balance of sweetness from scallops and caramel to sharpness from endives and lime juice.

This can be spoilt by undercooking the caramel in which case it will be too sweet, or by overcooking it which makes it bitter. Lift the pan from the heat as the sugar and butter mixture turns nut brown and add the endive before it blackens and starts to smell acrid.

If you are in doubt, then you may stop the caramelisation process with a few drops of water or fish stock before adding the endive.

Serves 4

12 scallops, white part only
2 Belgian endives (chicory)
2 lemons
1 lime
½ oz (15 g) butter
2 teaspoons white sugar
groundnut oil
salt and freshly ground black
   pepper

1.   You will need the lemon and lime zest which is easiest removed with a zesting knife. Failing this, cut the peel from the fruit in long strips; remove all pith, then slice into fine threads. Squeeze the lemons and lime. Pour half the juice into a small saucepan along with 2 fl oz (50 ml) water and the zested peel. Bring this to the boil and let it cool in the liquid.
2.   Separate the endives into individual leaves.
3.   Heat the butter and sugar together with three-quarters of the remaining juice. It will caramelise quite quickly. Add the endive, turning the leaves in the caramel. The endive will cook sufficiently in the caramel in the 4 or 5 minutes it takes to finish the dish.
4.   Slice the scallops into three horizontally. Turn them briefly on a plate with a teaspoonful of groundnut oil. Season with plenty of salt and black pepper.
5.   Heat a pan and quickly fry the scallops, about 30 seconds on each side will do. It will be easier to cook them in two batches, three if your pan is small, for it is important that they seal quickly.
6.   Heat enough oil to deep-fry the well-drained zest. Arrange a circle of caramelised endive on each plate. Pile the scallops on top.
7.   Deep-fry the zest for a few seconds, drain and scatter over the scallops. Finish the dish with the remaining drops of juice.

SCALLOP SALAD WITH SESAME DRESSING

Oils are acquiring the cachet of wine. Many Italian wineries also put their name to an olive oil and you may choose extra virgin, first cold pressing, filtered or unfiltered according to how you intend using it. The era of cabbage-lettuce and salad cream has given way to a rainbow of crisp leaves dressed in very specific oils and perhaps a balsamic vinegar 10 or 20 years old from Modena.

Walnut and sesame oils are travelling the same road, and sesame oil now comes either light so that you may fry with it or dark, from roast seeds, and intensely flavoured for dressings.

Just to complicate the issue I use a 50/50 combination of the two as I find the dark oil a shade too powerful.

The sesame dressing

1.   In a liquidiser, blend the pine kernels with the sesame oil, the lemon juice, soy sauce, ginger, coriander and white wine. In seconds this will emulsify into a dressing the consistency of single cream.

The scallops

All the observations on scallops attached to the recipe on page 55 apply. Basically very fresh scallops, and no prolonged contact with water.

2.   Clean and slice the scallops horizontally into three. Brush with a few drops of sesame oil and refrigerate until the moment they are to be cooked.

The salad

3.   Compose an interesting salad from the lettuces you have bought. The bitterness of the leaves should be a foil to the sweetness of the scallops.
4.   Toast the pine kernels and sprinkle them on top. Slice the tomatoes into strips and add them to the lettuces.

To complete

5.   Cook the scallops in a hot dry pan for a few seconds. Fry them in two or even three batches lest the volume of scallops reduces the pan heat to the extent that they bubble and boil instead of sealing instantly.
6.   Sprinkle sesame seeds across the scallops and remove from the pan.
7.   Drizzle 1 tablespoon of sesame oil across the salads. Squeeze a few drops of lemon on them also and, of course, a fine spray of salt. Spoon some sesame dressing around and across the salads and place the scallops wherever they look best.

Serves 4

12 scallops
sesame oil
a selection of salad leaves: lollo
   rosso, curly endive, oakleaf
   (*feuilles de chêne*), batavia
   and corn salad (*mâche*)
¼ oz (7.5 g) pine kernels
2 firm tomatoes, skinned and
   de-seeded

Sesame dressing
¼ oz (7.5 g) pine kernels
3 tablespoons sesame oil
juice of ½ lemon
1 teaspoon soy sauce
1 small knob ginger, peeled
   and chopped
1 sprig fresh coriander
1 tablespoon white wine

To complete
1 tablespoon sesame seeds
lemon juice
salt

Caviar on Potato Galette with Soured Cream and Chives

Caviar has associations of aged nobility and monocled generals eating in Edwardian surrounds served by butlers and maids. Luxury it certainly is, but a genuine one worth paying for on a special occasion.

This recipe gives a simple and delicious way to eat caviar. Traditionally, sieved boiled egg, chopped onion and lemon were served. These functioned to mask inferior or out of condition caviar and it amuses me to see the triumph on the occasional diner's face when he demands these 'proper' accompaniments.

Buy the best caviar you can afford. The best sturgeon come from the Caspian Sea. These are fished by the Russians and Iranians, but it is the Russians who have the reputation for quality. They only export top-grade caviar while the Iranians will also export second-grade.

The three sturgeons that produce real caviar are *beluga*, *ossietra* and *sevruga*. They are valuable creatures and are treated with the utmost care when netted, for a sturgeon when frightened releases a sour-tasting chemical into the roe. The *beluga* is the largest sturgeon and can weigh up to 1800 lb (810 kg) reaching 20 feet (6 metres) in length. The female must be 18 to 20 years old before she produces eggs. *Beluga* caviar, the largest grain and most delicate of the sturgeon eggs, has a smooth light taste and its colour varies from light to very dark grey. Small wonder it is the most expensive. *Ossietra* is also a large-grain caviar, and varies in colour sometimes taking on an almost yellow tinge. *Ossietra* sturgeon are smaller than *beluga*, weighing 100–200 lb (45–90 kg), and will also mature earlier at between 12 and 15 years. *Sevruga* sturgeon have a most distinctive shape with a long pointed muzzle in the form of a scythe. The *sevruga* matures early at seven years old and produces a medium-grain caviar. The colour again ranges from light to dark grey.

Caviar should be kept refrigerated until served. Unopened, the tins with their distinctive heavy rubber bands will keep fresh for a month. But, once opened, you should eat the caviar as soon as you can. Caviar should be spooned carefully from the tin so as not to break the eggs. Don't use a silver spoon, though, for the metal will impart a metallic taste.

The potato galettes

1. Peel the potatoes. Do not put them in water after they are peeled, for if you soak the starch out of them, the galettes will not stick together.
2. Grate the potatoes on the widest setting of your grater. Carefully season with nutmeg, salt and pepper.
3. Heat a little groundnut oil in a frying pan until it is quite hot.
4. Take a dessertspoonful of the potato, compress it briefly in your hand and place it into the frying pan. Let it become golden and crisp on each side, about 3–4 minutes each side. Pat dry on kitchen paper.

Serves 4

4 oz (100 g) caviar
5 fl oz (150 ml) soured cream
1 small bunch chives, snipped

Potato galettes
2 large potatoes
freshly grated nutmeg
salt and freshly ground black pepper
groundnut oil

To complete

5.   Place a potato galette in the centre of each plate.
6.   Mix the soured cream with the snipped chives. Spoon all round the potato galette. At the last moment spoon 1 oz (25 g) of caviar on top of each potato galette.

SALMON PAILLARD WITH LEMON AIOLI

A paillard is a cut of veal rather like a minute steak. The salmon for this dish is prepared in the same way, carved as thinly as possible, then flattened with a mallet between sheets of cling film. You are going to cook the salmon on plates and then drizzle the lemon and garlic sauce across the top. It is a method that uses very little fish and so makes a light, though tasty, meal when served with a tossed salad and some crusty white bread.

Traditional aïoli is a type of garlic mayonnaise made with a mortar and pestle. A liquidiser, however, will produce creditable results with less risk of the sauce curdling.

The lemon aïoli

1.   Blend all the ingredients except for the olive oil with ½ teaspoon salt and 1 teaspoon black pepper in a liquidiser or food processor.
2.   Pour the oil, in a trickle, into the sauce as it is blending. Add enough water – or fish stock if you have it – to thin the sauce to a pourable consistency. This will probably be about 2 tablespoons.

The salmon

3.   Carve the fish fillet into long thin slices, about ¼ in (6 mm) thick, each weighing around 3 oz (75 g). If this proves difficult, cut four 3 oz (75 g) fillets and carve each fillet straight down into four or five small slices and then proceed in exactly the same way.
4.   Place the fish between two sheets of cling film and tap it out, preferably with a mallet, to a thickness of ⅛ in (3 mm).
5.   Brush four heat-resistant plates with melted butter. Place them under a grill until hot. Season the salmon paillards with salt and pepper then put on to the hot plates.
6.   If the plates are hot enough the fish will cook with no other heat required and only need to be turned over before serving. Otherwise flash the plated salmon again under the grill for a few seconds.
7.   Trickle the lemon aïoli in a zig-zag across the salmon.

Serves 4

12 oz (350 g) salmon fillet (see method)
1 oz (25 g) butter, melted
salt and freshly ground black pepper

Lemon aïoli
2 egg yolks
4 garlic cloves
1 tablespoon fresh white breadcrumbs
juice of 1 lemon
10 fl oz (300 ml) olive oil

4

POULTRY AND GAME BIRDS

The duck family excepted, game birds and poultry are dry meats. Any roasting or grilling needs to be done with the addition of generous amounts of butter or oil, and any poaching has to be gentle, timed carefully to prevent overcooking.

Avoid battery chicken at all costs. It has no flavour, and should anyway offend your sensibilities. Reared game birds like pheasant or partridge are at least free-range, even if the concept of birds bred and raised to be shot as sport may seem a little comical. Truly wild creatures – woodcock, snipe and hare, for instance – have a much more pronounced flavour, and are thought of as an acquired taste.

Don't take any French chef's advice on game, for as a nation they have no real understanding of it. They don't hang game nearly long enough to allow a properly individual taste to develop, and compensate for the resulting toughness and lack of taste by marinating, a process which robs meat of its own flavour and substitutes the taste of wine vinegar and juniper berries.

Game dishes are often served with fruit-based sauces, usually some extension of redcurrant jelly. Presumably the reasoning behind this is similar to that of offering sweet biscuits, like digestives, with pungent cheese. However, I have never enjoyed these combinations so you will find no recipes for them here.

PAPRIKA CHICKEN WITH MARINATED CUCUMBER

Paprika is the key to this dish. Try to buy only as much as you need and don't keep opened packets of paprika for weeks as it loses flavour quickly and then has no more subtlety than brick dust.

In Hungary it is sold in four grades ranging in strength from quite mild rose paprika to the quite hot. As paprika available here is usually mild I have added a chilli to the ingredients. Creamy sauces need enlivening.

Paprika should fry for a few seconds, but mustn't burn or it will turn bitter. This is best accomplished by removing the pan from direct heat and then adding it. Added any other way paprika will taste uncooked – like a Frenchman's curry. You may then boil it forever without achieving the warmth and spiciness of the properly used product.

The cucumber salad which finishes the sauce also makes a good side dish with any braised meat or a rich stew and keeps well in the fridge for a few days.

Pilaff rice is ideal to serve with this dish for there is plenty of sauce to mop up. In Hungary you would probably be offered *galuska*, an eastern European *spaetzle* made by rubbing thickish batter through a colander into boiling water. However this is not the moment for such touches of authenticity. Concentrate on the paprika chicken with marinated cucumber.

The cucumber salad

Serves 4

1 × 4 lb (1.75 kg) chicken
1 large onion, peeled and chopped
1 tablespoon groundnut oil
1 tablespoon paprika
1 small chilli, chopped
1 teaspoon tomato purée
1 large red pepper, de-seeded and chopped
1 tablespoon arrowroot
5 fl oz (150 ml) crème fraîche

Cucumber salad
1 cucumber
1 teaspoon salt
1 teaspoon sugar
1 tablespoon white wine vinegar
black pepper

1. Peel and thinly slice the cucumber. Sprinkle the salt over the slices. You will now need to press the cucumber, and the easiest method is to place an upturned plate over it, put a 2 lb (900 g) weight on top, and then leave for 1 hour. Remove the weight and squeeze as much liquid as you can from the cucumber.
2. Dissolve the sugar and vinegar together with a few turns of the pepper mill. Add the cucumber and refrigerate until needed.

The chicken

3. In a pot large enough to hold the chicken, fry the onion in the oil until brown. Add the paprika, then the chopped chilli and tomato purée. Allow these to fry for a few seconds then pour on a pint (600 ml) of water. Bring to the boil and then add the chicken and red pepper.
4. Cover the pot with a tight-fitting lid. Lower the heat so that the chicken is gently poached for 40 minutes by which time it should be perfectly cooked. Lift it out.
5. Thicken the paprika stock with the arrowroot diluted in a little cold water. Add the crème fraîche, re-boil, and then strain into a clean saucepan.

To complete

6.   Carve the chicken into eight pieces; the two legs and breasts each divided into two. Return these pieces to the paprika sauce.
7.   Lift the cucumber salad from its marinade and add this to the sauce.
8.   Serve each person a piece of leg and breast and plenty of sauce.

'BOURRIDE' OF CHICKEN THICKENED WITH GARLIC MAYONNAISE

Bourride is a garlicky fish soup from the Mediterranean. Chicken given the same treatment is even better.

The garlic mayonnaise

Serves 4

1 × 4 lb (1.8 kg) chicken
salt and freshly ground black
   pepper
4 shallots, peeled
1 leek, trimmed
5 fl oz (150 ml) white wine
1 pinch saffron

Garlic mayonnaise
8 garlic cloves, peeled
2 egg yolks
1 teaspoon Dijon mustard
2 teaspoons white wine vinegar
2½ fl oz (65 ml) olive oil
2½ fl oz (65 ml) groundnut oil

1.   Crush the garlic. The best way to do this is to sprinkle a little salt on each clove, then press it with the flat of the blade of a heavy knife, which turns it quickly to pulp.
2.   Whisk the egg yolks, garlic, mustard, vinegar and a little salt and pepper together. Gradually whisk in both of the oils.

The chicken

3.   Use a heavy ovenproof casserole or pot, preferably cast-iron, which will hold the whole chicken. Season the chicken with salt and pepper and put it in the chosen pot.
4.   Add the shallots and leek to the pot. Pour on the white wine, the pinch of saffron and add a pint (600 ml) of cold water.
5.   Bring to the boil. Cover tightly, put the pot into a moderately hot oven – 375°F (190°C) Gas 5 – and cook for about 45 minutes.

To complete

6.   Remove the chicken from the liquor and carve it into eight pieces – two thighs, two drumsticks and four half breasts.
7.   Whisk the garlic mayonnaise into the cooking liquor. You cannot re-boil the sauce after this or it will separate.
8.   Put the chicken pieces on to a serving dish and strain the thickened cooking liquor over them. It is best eaten from large soup bowls with wild rice pilaff (see page 26).

ROAST CHICKEN WITH WATERCRESS AND APRICOT STUFFING

As a general rule I dislike combinations of meat or fish and fruit. The apricot in this stuffing is an exception, adding moistness and lift to both stuffing and chicken.

Most people consider themselves expert at jobs like roast chicken or scrambled egg. A little humility in approach to this dish will improve results more than any chef's tip.

The stuffing

1. Convert the bread into crumbs with a food processor. Bring the apricots to the boil in a small saucepan of water; drain them and then add to the breadcrumbs. Roughly chop the watercress and hazelnuts, then add these also.
2. Process these ingredients together for a few seconds and then scrape out the resulting stuffing base into a bowl.

The salt and pepper

3. In a small dry frying pan cook the salt and peppercorns together. Use a low heat and toss the pan frequently so that they cook evenly. This will take 10 minutes and can be done in an oven if you prefer (the same temperature as below). Grind the pepper and salt together in an electric mill or alternatively with a pestle and mortar.

The chicken and stuffing

4. Sprinkle the chicken with half the roast pepper and salt. Leave the butter to soften slightly, then spread it generously over the chicken. Roast in a moderately hot oven – 375°F (190°C) Gas 5 – for an hour, until completely cooked.

Cook the chicken on its side, turning the bird over after half an hour. The aim is to protect the breast meat from the fiercer heat as it is more tender and tends to dry out.
5. At this midway point, when turning the bird, pour 3 tablespoons of the sizzling butter in the roasting tray on to the stuffing base you have made. Mix it in completely. Roll the stuffing in foil so that it is sausage shaped, like a small salami, and put this into the roasting tray with the chicken for the remaining cooking time.

Serves 4

1 × 3–4 lb (1.3–1.75 kg) free-range chicken
1 tablespoon coarse sea salt
1 tablespoon black peppercorns
8 oz (225 g) unsalted butter

Stuffing
4 slices white bread
2 oz (50 g) dried apricots
1 small bunch watercress
2 oz (50 g) hazelnuts

Rack of lamb with parsley served with jabron potatoes, stir-fried carrots and mange-touts.

Fillet steak with celeriac and morel mushrooms, here pictured in a coppice by the river.

Bresaola – home cured beef – with some poached leeks in mustard and olive oil dressing.

Foie gras salad, along with brioche and a glass of wine, is all you need for a spring picnic amongst the crocuses in front of Gidleigh Park.

Poppyseed parfait with plum sauce.

Caramel and apple tart with caramel ice cream.

A Devon cream tea on a dull afternoon in the drawing room. Also pictured are a chocolate fudge cake, syrup and oatmeal biscuits, shortbread and morning biscuits.

The day's baking. Buttermilk rolls, granary and soda breads, croissants and brioche,
poppyseed rolls and hazelnut bread.

To complete

6.   Lift the stuffing and chicken on to a large plate to rest. Pour away the buttery fat and deglaze the roasting tray – a useful term for boiling out residual flavours from pans which have been used for frying or roasting – with 10 fl oz (300 ml) of water. Boil this down by half and add any meat juices from the chicken which accumulate on the plate.

7.   Carve the chicken into joints, not slices. Start by cutting away each leg and splitting them into thighs and drumsticks. Next cut away the breast from each side of the carcass, and halve them. Finally turn the bird over and take out the two oysters of tender meat that lie midway along the backbone.

8.   Serve each person a piece of leg and a piece of breast, a spoonful of stuffing and a spoonful of the unthickened gravy. Offer the remaining roast pepper and salt.

GRESSINGHAM DUCK WITH GARLIC AND SHALLOT CONFIT AND SAUTERNES SAUCE

Gressingham ducks are a relatively new variety developed in northern England from mallards. They are small, lean animals which provide dark, steak-like meat not dissimilar to French Challans ducks. As with French varieties Gressingham ducks are best served pink. Their advantage is that they are more tender than the Challans.

Mine are raised, under licence, on a farm near Bodmin in Cornwall, but they are becoming quite widely available around the country.

Serves 4

2 Gressingham ducks
20 garlic cloves, peeled
12 small shallots, peeled
4 fl oz (120 ml) milk
1 oz (25 g) unsalted butter
salt and freshly ground black pepper
4 fl oz (120 ml) Sauternes
8 fl oz (250 ml) veal sauce base (see page 120)

1.   Boil the garlic cloves and shallots in the milk for 4 minutes, then drain and thoroughly dry with kitchen paper. Wrap in silver foil with a knob of butter ready for cooking with the ducks.

2.   Season the ducks with salt and pepper and place them in a roasting tray along with the foil parcel of garlic and shallots.

3.   Roast for 30 minutes in an oven preheated to 450°F (230°C), Gas 8. Remove the ducks from the oven. Carve off the legs and return them to the oven for a further 10 minutes' cooking while the breasts rest.

To complete

4.   Now take out the duck legs and the foil packet with garlic and shallots. Empty the roasting tray of fat and pour in first the Sauternes and then the veal sauce base. Bring this to the boil, then strain into a jug.

5.   Carve the breasts into slivers and lay these on the plates along with the legs and confit vegetables. Pour the sauce around the duck.

Aylesbury Duckling, Steamed and Crisp-fried, and Served with Salad

Never confuse the Aylesbury or Chinese variety of ducks with Barbary or other lean ducks. The native variety has delicious skin, a small but tender layer of pale meat, and quite a lot of fat. It suits roasting and steaming. Barbary ducks (or Challans ducks from France and, to a lesser extent, Gressingham ducks) have a thick, dark breast, and skin which is unpleasant to eat. These are best treated like steaks and served underdone.

The duck

Serves 4

1 × 6 lb (2.75 kg) Aylesbury duckling
salt and freshly ground black pepper
4 tablespoons groundnut oil

1.   Take out the wishbone. This forms an arch around the base of the bird's neck which you can feel if you run your finger along it. Remove it by lifting back the flap of neck skin to expose the meat, and then cutting the bone out. It is easier to dismantle the duck after steaming if the wishbone is out.
2.   Mill plenty of salt and black pepper over the bird, wrap in foil and steam for 1½ hours. Use a steamer or a large covered saucepan with a little water in the bottom, in which case you will need to rest the duck on a grid to keep it clear of the water. You will also have to check the water level periodically lest it runs dry.
3.   Unwrap the foil and pour the clear cooking juices into a container for use in the dressing.

Cassis dressing
1 tablespoon white wine vinegar
1 teaspoon Crème de Cassis
5 tablespoons olive oil

The Cassis dressing

Salad
1 frisée
4 small bunches corn salad (*mâche*)
1 lollo rosso
4 spring onions

4.   Mix the vinegar, Cassis and a tablespoon of the duck's cooking juices (keep the rest of this – it freezes well and is useful for sauces or soup). Whisk in the olive oil, and season with salt and pepper.

The sweetness of the Cassis should be 'balanced' by the vinegar. The cooking juices from the duck dilute the dressing so that it remains an emulsion – not separating back into components – and to help you eat more of it!

The salad

5.   Wash the lettuces in plenty of cold water. Shake dry and separate into leaves. Trim the spring onions.

To complete

6.   Cut the duck into four joints: two legs and thighs and two breasts. Try not to tear the skin, which will be quite fragile.
7.   Heat the groundnut oil in a frying pan. Fry the duck pieces skin side down until they are crisp and brown. Lift them on to kitchen paper to drain for a few seconds.
8.   Place the salads around the edges of four cold plates, dipping each leaf briefly into a saucer of the dressing. Leftover dressing can be poured into the centre of each plate. Season the salad with a little salt, and put a piece of crisp hot duck into the middle of it. Serve straightaway – the salad will wilt if you wait.

ROAST WOODCOCK ON TOAST

The arrival of woodcock in late autumn is not heralded with the pantomime which greets the first grouse on the 12th of August. Nonetheless it is an aristocrat amongst game birds. Its dark rich flesh is better if hung for a week, and there is the bonus of delicious offal.

Don't let the unappetising sight of woodcock devotees consuming the brains dissuade you from doing likewise. They are a delicacy.

Snipe are treated in much the same way except that they are small enough to grill, like chops. A gravy made from pan juice is the only sauce you need.

Serves 4

4 woodcock
8 oz (225 g) unsalted butter
4 slices white bread
½ lemon
1 teaspoon cognac
salt and freshly ground black
    pepper

1.   Spread the butter generously over the woodcock breasts.
2.   Roast the birds for 20 minutes at 400°F (200°C) Gas 6. Toast the bread.
3.   You will need to remove the innards at this stage, I'm afraid. Spoon them into a saucepan and mash them with a fork. They will be barely cooked so heat them through with a few drops of lemon juice, the cognac, and salt and pepper. Spread this paste on the toast.
4.   Carve the birds into breasts and legs. Take the tip of a sharp knife and split the heads. Assemble the woodcock on the toast, legs followed by breasts and the two halves of the head on top.
5.   Serve with braised lentils and winter salads.

CORN-FED PIGEON WITH VEGETABLES AND OLIVE OIL SAUCE

These pigeons, which are frequently sold under their American name 'squab', are reared specifically for the table. They handle differently from wood pigeons and are reliably tender, even the legs.

You will need a blender for the sauce. Stock-based sauces or dressings, like this one, will not incorporate enough olive oil to influence the flavour without some centrifugal force.

The vegetables

This recipe is for early summer. At other times of year use different vegetables. If the carrots or leeks are woody, substitute whatever is in peak condition, perhaps salsify or French beans.

1. Wash the vegetables, trimming and peeling where necessary. If the carrots are large, cut them into 1 in (2.5 cm) lengths, likewise the leeks and asparagus.
2. Bring the sauce stock to the boil, and poach the vegetables. Add them in the order of how long they take to cook – carrots first, then asparagus, leeks and mange-touts. Lift out these vegetables and then separately boil the spinach for 1 minute. Lift this out to drain well.

The pigeons and sauce

3. Brush a little olive oil on to the pigeons. Season with salt and pepper. Roast them in a hot oven – 400°F (200°C) Gas 6 – for about 20 minutes.

They will be cooked pink which is how I like them. If you prefer pigeon well done leave them in the oven for another 15 minutes.
4. Deglaze the roasting pan with the poaching stock from the vegetables. Add the shallot, garlic and then the cream. Pour this into a liquidiser and blend. As it blends, slowly pour in the olive oil.

To complete

5. Place a little spinach on each of four warmed plates. Make a small pile of vegetables on top. Carve the pigeon into two breasts and two legs each. Place these on the mounds of vegetables and pour round the warm olive oil sauce.

Serves 4

4 corn-fed pigeons
2 lb (900 g) young carrots
4 small leeks
4 asparagus spears
8 oz (225 g) mange-touts
1 lb (450 g) spinach, washed, tough stalks removed
olive oil
salt and freshly ground black pepper

Sauce
10 fl oz (300 ml) chicken stock (see page 30)
1 shallot, peeled and chopped
1 garlic clove, peeled
2 tablespoons double cream
5 fl oz (150 ml) virgin olive oil

GRILLED GUINEA FOWL WITH BRAISED CHESTNUTS

The appreciation of chestnuts came to me only recently. They are rather sweet and a nuisance to shell. Luckily they are now available vacuum packed. Their flavour marries well with spices like mace and nutmeg in pheasant or guinea fowl dishes.

Serves 4

2 × 2 lb (900 g) guinea fowl
groundnut oil

Braised chestnuts
8 peeled chestnuts
12 pickling onions, peeled
12 small carrots, peeled
2 rashers streaky bacon
½ teaspoon ground mace
salt and freshly ground black
   pepper
2 fl oz (50 ml) sieved tomato
   (passata)
2 fl oz (50 ml) red wine
a sprig of fresh thyme

The birds

1.   Divide the guinea fowl into breast fillets and legs. Chop the carcasses in two.
2.   Remove the skin from the breasts and lightly bat them out between sheets of cling film. You don't need to bat them until they are thin but just until they are of even thickness. This is because you will want to grill them until they are just done but still moist and juicy inside rather than having the edges overcooked and dry and the thicker, shoulder area undercooked.
3.   Brush with oil and refrigerate until later.

The braised chestnuts

4.   Heat a heavy casserole and fry the guinea fowl carcasses and legs, onions, carrots and bacon in 2 tablespoons groundnut oil until they start to colour.
5.   Add mace, salt and pepper, then stir in the sieved tomato – sold commercially as passata – and red wine. Pour in 7 fl oz (200 ml) of cold water and bring to the boil.
6.   Cut the chestnuts into quarters and add, with the thyme. Cover with a lid and cook these ingredients either in a moderate oven at 350°F (180°C) Gas 4, or over a low heat, for about half an hour.

To complete

7.   Fish out the vegetables, chestnuts and any tender, cooked leg meat. Put these into a clean saucepan and strain the cooking liquors over them.
8.   Season the oiled breasts and grill them, preferably on a charcoal barbecue. They will cook quickly, 7 or 8 minutes.
9.   Serve the grilled breast against the braised chestnut and vegetables.

QUAIL SALAD WITH WARM WALNUT DRESSING

Warm salads are no longer particularly fashionable. Like quiche, pâtés and terrines they have moved along the conveyor belt of over-use into new oblivion. Perhaps they must wait a while like soups to be suddenly rediscovered. You and I need have no such worries. A warm salad – salad with warm components, to be more precise – offers contrasts of hot and cold, crunchiness of lettuces against meat or fish, and the opportunity to use an interesting dressing.

This quail salad is designed to be a first course. With more lettuce and some good bread it would make a perfectly satisfactory lunch.

1.   Wash and dry all the lettuces.
2.   Grill the bacon and chop it. Toast the pine kernels.
3.   Seal the quails in the groundnut oil in a hot ovenproof metal pan, then put the pan and quails into a hot oven preheated to 400°F (200°C) Gas 6 for 15 minutes so that they are cooked.
4.   Make the lettuces into four crisp salads. Sprinkle 1 tablespoon of the walnut oil and 1 teaspoon of the balsamic vinegar over the leaves. Season with salt.
5.   Carve the quails into legs and breasts. Tuck these and the bacon and pine kernels in the salads.

To complete

6.   Deglaze the quail pan with 5 fl oz (150 ml) cold water, the remaining walnut oil and vinegar. As it boils it will emulsify like a sauce.
7.   Pour this hot dressing around each salad.

Serves 4

4 quails
a selection of salad leaves: lollo
    rosso, corn salad (*mâche*),
    frisée, cos or little gem
    lettuce
2 rashers streaky bacon
1 tablespoon pine kernels
1 tablespoon groundnut oil
2 tablespoons walnut oil
2 teaspoons balsamic vinegar
a pinch of salt

BUTCHER'S MEAT

Whatever the trend towards healthy eating, vegetarianism and the like, meat is traditionally the centre of any meal, the part first decided when planning a meal, and the part around which all else is built.

The role of the cook is technical rather than creative – astute purchase, and the choice of cooking method most suited to the joint. Because you have budgeted for topside of beef and would like a roast dinner doesn't necessarily mean that roast topside is a good dish: braised or pot-roasted topside would be better (and a forerib would make an ideal roast). The cook's objective is to make the best, most appropriate, use of the meat and it is paradoxical that most skill and creativity is needed to cook cheaper, less exalted cuts. With best Scottish sirloin or saddle of lamb you have only to avoid a major mishap for success, and the major skill is finding the large amounts of cash necessary to buy them.

Meat generally means red meat, beef or lamb. Pork still has associations with poverty – though strangely ham and bacon do not – and veal is rarely eaten at all.

Where are the pitfalls in meat cookery? The greatest potential for disaster involves fanciful combinations of meat with fish or fruit, demented marriages of lamb with shellfish sauce or worse. All very well that oysters are traditionally popped into beef-steak pies and redcurrant sauce served with lamb – you keep well clear of untried territory.

This area is a minefield littered with bad meals made from good ingredients. Be conservative. Mustard, red wine, mushrooms, the judicious use of herbs and spices, these are the key. Don't impose any unlikely combinations on your friends or family because it looks attractive on the plate. You have first courses, soups, vegetables and puddings to show your deft hand with the kitchen equipment.

There is also the question of how long meat should be cooked – roast and grilled meat that is. I don't think there is any argument over stew. Well done prime meat may produce better gravy, but this is rather a waste of money when braising will produce more succulent results from cheaper cuts. My own preference is for rare meat but if I am at someone else's table and am served something more cooked, I can of course eat it even if it is less enjoyable. People who eat meat well done, on the other hand, appear to become revolted and frightened by the prospect of rareness. It is for you to judge your guests' preferences.

BOILED KNUCKLE OF VEAL

Veal is dull meat most famous as a vehicle for fried breadcrumbs in *Wiener Schnitzel*. Knuckle is the calf equivalent of beef shin. It is much more tender than shin but still quite gelatinous, and is excellent boiled or braised. Aside from its offal, this is my favourite cut of veal.

It is not an ideal restaurant dish. The meat takes too long to cook. We have to adapt it by making the stock separately and then poaching very tender cuts, like loin, a portion at a time. The mechanics of restaurant kitchen cooking, where a party of six people are liable to order different dishes at each course and expect to sit down to eat 10 minutes later, mean that each menu item must be dismantled like Lego into component jobs that can be done in advance and brought together swiftly as ordered. You need to be able to cook meat or fish in 10 or 15 minutes so only prime cuts are really appropriate.

Good dishes like this or a spring lamb stew are better made at home than in a restaurant. At home you are wise enough to offer no choice and decide what time dinner will be served. Actually there are no conjuring tricks to restaurant cooking, merely the facility which comes of doing the job regularly. Behind the scenes, in my experience, is regularly like Fawlty Towers and occasionally Bates Motel.

Serves 4

1 knuckle of veal
1 calf's foot
2 large carrots, peeled
1 lb (450 g) potatoes, peeled
1 lb (450 g) small onions or shallots, peeled
½ Savoy cabbage, cut into largish cubes
4 oz (100 g) piece of streaky bacon
a sprig of fresh thyme
ground black pepper

1.   Find a pot or casserole that is large enough to hold the veal knuckle. In it heat just enough water to cover the joint. You will not need any salt.
2.   Split the calf's foot lengthwise and add it to the pot.
3.   When the water comes to the boil, put in the veal knuckle, fit a lid and let the veal simmer for an hour.
4.   Add all the vegetables, except the cabbage, plus the piece of bacon. Continue cooking.
5.   After 20 minutes add the cabbage. The objective is that all the ingredients finish cooking simultaneously. Add the sprig of thyme and some black pepper.
6.   About 10 minutes later check that all the vegetables are cooked and, provided that they indeed are, lift them out of the stock, along with the meat.

To complete

7.   Carve the meat into slices and place it with the vegetables in four large soup dishes. Ladle some cooking stock into each bowl. Serve mustard or horseradish separately.

Home-cured Beef (Bresaola) with Baby Leeks

This Italian dish is similar to eastern Switzerland's *Bunderfleisch*. Lean joints like topside or rump work best. The basis of the recipe was given to me by Franco Taruschio who makes it particularly well in his Welsh restaurant, The Walnut Tree at Llandewi Skirrid, near Abergavenny.

There is no point in making two or three portions of *bresaola* at a time. Make plenty; it keeps for ages, hanging, or once trimmed, in the fridge – treat it like salami or Parma ham. The marinating and hanging times are based on a 4 lb (1.8 kg) piece of topside, the way you would most likely receive it from the butcher. If you buy a smaller or a particularly thin joint, the whole process will take less time, but I would recommend that you consider multiplying the quantities by two or four times.

About a dozen main-course servings

1 × 4 lb (1.8 kg) piece of beef topside
3 lb (1.3 kg) small leeks
olive oil

Brine
½ bottle red wine
1 lb (450 g) salt
¼ oz (7.5 g) saltpetre
4 oz (100 g) brown sugar
1 tablespoon black peppercorns, crushed
1 tablespoon juniper berries, crushed
1 sprig fresh thyme
8 oz (225 g) carrots, sliced
6 chillies
1 cinnamon stick

Dressing
1 egg yolk
1 tablespoon Dijon mustard
2 tablespoons sherry vinegar
salt and freshly ground black pepper
5 fl oz (150 ml) good olive oil

The meat

1. Combine the brine ingredients with a pint (600 ml) of water, bring to the boil and allow the mixture to cool.
2. Find the right-sized container – a small plastic bucket or a deep tray. Place the joint in the container and pour the brine over it. Leave this to marinate for 4 days. If the meat isn't completely covered, turn it every day.
3. Lift the meat from the brine, pat dry with kitchen paper or a clean dry cloth, wrap in muslin or cheesecloth, and hang in a dry warm place for 2 weeks (3 if a large joint), or until quite firm when pressed with your finger. It is best hanging away from the wall so that air can circulate around it.
4. The outside of the joint will look awful, particularly if you have not wrapped it in muslin. Carefully cut away the dried outside layer and you will be left with a deep purple block.

The dressing

5. Whisk the egg yolk with mustard, then whisk in the vinegar and some salt and pepper.
6. Add the olive oil slowly, beating all of the time. This should give you an emulsified dressing. If it is a little thick add a few drops of water. When you taste for seasoning it should be fine unless you have done something wrong.

To complete

7. Poach the baby leeks in salted water for about 2 minutes. Cut them into 2 in (5 cm) lengths and turn them over in the dressing.
8. Slice the *bresaola* as thinly as you can. If you don't have a good slicing machine, it may help to put it into a freezer for an hour or so.
9. Cover a plate with these thin slices. Grind a little black pepper across it, and sprinkle with olive oil. Spoon a bundle of the dressed baby leeks on to this and serve with hot bread.

Fillet Steak with Celeriac and Morel Mushrooms

Wild mushrooms, especially morels, and celeriac marry well, and I start to think of dishes like this when autumn approaches. I use fillet steak regularly in this combination, but it also complements venison and hare well.

For sauces, I prefer dried morels and ceps (which you may know as *boletus* or *porcini*) to fresh ones, because they give a more intense flavour.

You need to make stock for this dish; pan juices will not suffice. Making stock creates a number of dirty pans disproportionate to the amount of liquid obtained. There is no short cut; bouillon cubes won't do. When I make stock at home I always double or quadruple the quantity and freeze what's left for another day.

The mushrooms

1.   Soak the mushrooms for an hour or two in cold water, then slice them in half lengthwise and wash them thoroughly. Remove the stalks and use them in the stock.

The stock

2.   Roast the bones in a moderate oven – 350°F (180°C) Gas 4 – for 30 minutes, then add the diced vegetables, garlic, tomato and the stalks from the morels. Continue to roast until they are brown, about 45 minutes altogether.

3.   Using a slotted spoon, lift the bones and vegetables from the roasting tray into a large saucepan. Discard the fat from the pan, deglaze it with 10 fl oz (300 ml) water, then pour this and a further 3½ pints (2 litres) of cold water into the pan. Bring to the boil, turn down the heat and simmer gently for 2 hours. Skim off periodically any scum that rises to the surface.

4.   Strain the stock – which will probably now be about 1½–2 pints (900 ml – 1.2 litres) – into a clean saucepan and reduce gently until you have about 10 fl oz (300 ml) left.

The celeriac

5.   Peel the celeriac with a small, sharp knife and split in half. Cut one half into cubes and the other into thin strips.

6.   Boil the cubes in salt water until tender, about 15 minutes. Drain, and mash or process through a blender. Season with salt and pepper, and add the cream.

7.   Pan-fry the celeriac strips in the butter for 3 or 4 minutes, until golden brown.

Serves 4

4 × 6 oz (175 g) fillet steaks
1 oz (25 g) dried morel
   mushrooms
1 × 3 lb (1.3 kg) celeriac
salt and freshly ground black
   pepper
4 fl oz (120 ml) double cream
1 oz (25 g) unsalted butter
1 teaspoon olive oil

Veal stock
1 lb (450 g) veal bones, chopped
1 onion, peeled and diced
1 carrot, scrubbed and diced
1 leek, trimmed and diced
1 garlic clove
2 oz (50 g) tomato passata or
   sun-dried tomato

To complete

8.   Brush the steaks with the olive oil, then pan-fry them. A copper pan would be ideal but an iron skillet will substitute; in either case it should be preheated so that the meat seals. You'll need about 4 minutes each side for medium rare. Lift the steaks from the pan and keep them warm.

9.   Deglaze the pan with the stock and add the morels. Boil until the liquid thickens, about 2 minutes.

10.   Put a good spoonful of celeriac purée on each plate. Place a fillet steak on top of this. Put a spoonful of celeriac strips on top of each steak, then spoon the dark morel sauce around it.

Streaky Pork with Grated Marrow and Dill

The marrow and dill confection derives from a Hungarian dish called *Tok Fozelek*. It tastes fresh and has a little sharpness that partners the sweetness of belly pork very well.

The consistency of the marrow acts as a sauce as well as a vegetable.

The marrow

Serves 4

1½ lb (675 g) belly pork
5 lb (2.25 kg) vegetable marrow
salt
1 small onion, peeled and
    chopped
1 garlic clove, peeled and
    crushed
2 oz (50 g) lard
1 small bunch (1½ oz/40 g)
    fresh dill
1 oz (25 g) plain flour
10 fl oz (300 ml) soured cream
1 teaspoon malt vinegar
freshly ground black pepper

1.   Peel the marrow and then cut it into matchstick-sized threads. If you have a vegetable mandoline or food processor attachment, then use it.

2.   Sprinkle the marrow with a teaspoonful of salt and leave it for half an hour. Squeeze out the brine which forms.

3.   Fry the onion and crushed garlic without colouring, in the lard. Add 5 fl oz (150 ml) cold water and then the dill and marrow. Bring to the boil.

4.   Mix the flour and soured cream, then thicken the marrow with it. Let the thickened marrow boil gently for 10 minutes, taking care that it doesn't stick to the pan and burn. Finish the marrow with a little vinegar and ground pepper. Check whether it needs salt. Keep warm.

The pork

5.   Meanwhile, cut the pork into eight slices. Remove the rind. Sprinkle with salt and pepper, then grill until crisp on both sides, around half an hour.

To complete

6.   Spread a good portion of the marrow on each plate and place two slices of crisp pork on top.

NOISETTES OF VENISON WITH FOIE GRAS AND MADEIRA SAUCE

Venison is an overworked word that has to do duty for the meat of anything antlered. Generally it means the flesh of red, fallow or roe deer. There is little point asking the butcher which is on offer any more than enquiring which breed of lamb or beef is on the slab. Yet they are different in several respects: size, tenderness and taste.

Recently killed venison doesn't taste much different from recently killed beef. Its flavour develops and matures with hanging. Really well hung venison is magnificent and never needs marinating. You may have to shave off the outer layer of a particularly ripe joint, but it will be worth it for the superior texture and taste.

The venison in this dish is cooked like Tournedos Rossini, with foie gras and Madeira sauce. Use the eye of the meat from the saddle. The bones will make a gamey Madeira sauce.

The sauce

1.   Take the saddle bones and chop them into small, maybe ½ in (1 cm), pieces. Fry them in a little oil in a large saucepan until they are brown. Fry the vegetables and, as they brown, add the tomato purée, letting it fry for a few seconds. Add 1 pint (600 ml) of cold water and bring to the boil.
2.   Skim off any surface scum and then simmer the stock for 30 minutes. Strain the stock into a small saucepan and re-boil. Moisten the arrowroot with a few drops of the Madeira, and lightly thicken the sauce with it. Add the remaining Madeira.

The venison and foie gras

3.   Cut the venison fillet into eight 2 oz (50 g) noisettes. Season them with salt and pepper.
4.   Brush the noisettes with oil and fry in a hot pan. I prefer it medium rare, about 2 minutes each side, but you cook it as you wish.
5.   Clean the pan with kitchen paper, then fry the foie gras briefly on both sides. Lift out on to kitchen paper. Pour off the fat from the pan and add the Madeira sauce. Let it boil a few seconds, then whisk in the butter and strain into a jug.

To complete

6.   Toast the bread, then cut it into the shape of the noisettes.
7.   Assemble thus. If you are serving any green vegetable like spinach, use it as a base. Place two pieces of toast on each plate. Then the noisettes of venison. Then the foie gras. Lastly the sauce.

Serves 4

1 lb (450 g) venison fillet, cut
   from the saddle
groundnut oil
4 oz (100 g) duck foie gras
salt and freshly ground black
   pepper
4 slices white bread

Sauce
venison bones
1 onion, peeled and chopped
1 leek, trimmed and chopped
1 carrot, peeled and chopped
1 teaspoon tomato purée
½ teaspoon arrowroot
2 fl oz (50 ml) Malmsey Madeira
1 oz (25 g) unsalted butter

RACK OF LAMB WITH PARSLEY

This dish needs no sauce but goes extremely well with a creamy potato dish like Gratin de Jabron (see page 25).

A small amount of fat left on the bones will sweeten the meat and heighten its lamb flavour. Lamb is available year round but is at its best in early summer. Better than new season's lamb which is overrated and vastly superior to milk-fed lamb which is virtually tasteless.

The meat

Serves 4

1 pair best ends of lamb
salt and freshly ground black
  pepper
2 tablespoons Dijon mustard

Stuffing
4 oz (100 g) unsalted butter
4 shallots, peeled and chopped
a bunch of parsley, chopped
8 oz (225 g) fresh breadcrumbs

Good butchery will make carving the finished joint much easier. Ask the butcher when he splits the best ends into two racks to chop either side of the chine bone rather than through it.

1. Lift off the outer layer of skin and fat. It comes away easily and in one piece. The eye of meat will now be exposed but covered in a white gristly membrane. Take a sharp knife and remove this. Chop down the cutlet bones so they extend no more than 3 in (7.5 cm) from the eye of the meat.
2. Season with salt and pepper. Preheat the oven to 425°F (220°C) Gas 7.

The stuffing

3. Melt the butter in a saucepan. When it has melted, but before it colours, add the shallots then the parsley and breadcrumbs.
4. Season with some salt and pepper and stir together to form a stuffing.

To complete

5. Seal the meat in a hot pan, then roast in the preheated oven for 7 minutes.
6. Brush the racks with mustard then pack the parsley stuffing over them.
7. Brown under a hot grill. Carve into cutlets and serve.

LAMB HAMBURGER WITH GARLIC AND PEPPER

I ate something rather like this at Stars restaurant in San Francisco. Americans do not appear to eat lamb in the quantity we do, so a dish this simple and good was a surprise; a tribute to the inventive talent of Jeremiah Tower, the chef-proprietor of Stars.

1.   Poach the whole garlic cloves in 10 fl oz (300 ml) water until tender, about 15 minutes.
2.   Crush the peppercorns in a mortar and pestle or grind them very coarsely in a mill.
3.   Salt the lamb, which should have at least some fat, and press it into four hamburgers. Roll them in the cracked pepper.
4.   Heat a frying pan. Brush the hamburgers with olive oil and then cook them briefly, around 2 minutes on each side. They should still be rare. Place a lamb hamburger on each warmed plate.
5.   Deglaze the frying pan with the garlic and its cooking liquor. Add the tomato, coriander and butter. Shake the pan to amalgamate the melting butter.
6.   Spoon the sauce over the lamb, and serve with salad.

Serves 4

1½ lb (675 g) lamb, minced
12 garlic cloves
2 tablespoons black
   peppercorns
salt
1 teaspoon olive oil
2 tomatoes, skinned, de-seeded
   and chopped
1 sprig fresh coriander,
   chopped
1 oz (25 g) unsalted butter

RABBIT AND MUSTARD RAGOUT

A classic combination. Serve it with fresh tagliatelle and, in November, a few shavings of white truffle.

Rabbit has overcome its poor image during the last few years. I use farmed rabbit rather than wild because the offal is so superior. It has a clean yet distinctive taste and, provided you don't overcook it, will be moist and tender.

What was it that distressed people at the thought of eating rabbit? Was it myxomatosis? The idea of consuming Bugs Bunny? Poor Bambi doesn't seem to curb venison sales, and swine vesicular disease hasn't altered the popularity of bacon. One of life's mysteries, perhaps, not for us to understand.

The rabbit

Serves 4

1 farmed rabbit
salt and freshly ground black
    pepper
groundnut oil

Stock

1 onion, peeled and chopped
1 leek, washed and chopped
1 carrot, scraped and chopped
2 fl oz (50 ml) white wine
1 teaspoon arrowroot

Sauce

1 tablespoon Dijon mustard
5 fl oz (150 ml) double cream
1 fl oz (25 ml) olive oil
2 oz (50 g) Pecorino or
    Parmesan cheese, grated

1.   Firstly joint it into two front, two hind legs and the main saddle containing two long fillets on top and the liver and kidneys in the cavity underneath. Cut out these fillets and the offal. Lift all membrane from the fillets and hind legs, then remove the bone from each of the hind legs. Cut the meat into large – 1 in (2.5 cm) – cubes.
2.   Chop the carcass and front legs for the stock.

The stock

3.   Place the chopped vegetables and the rabbit carcass and front legs into a roasting tray, and then roast in a hot oven – 400°F (200°C) Gas 6 – for about 30 minutes until brown.
4.   Lift these bones and vegetables from the roasting tray into a medium-sized saucepan. Throw out any grease from the roasting tray and then deglaze with white wine and 10 fl oz (300 ml) cold water. Pour this liquor and a further 1½ pints (900 ml) water into the saucepan with the bones. Bring this to the boil and simmer for 2 hours.
5.   Strain into a smaller saucepan and reduce until only 5 fl oz (150 ml) remains. Thicken this with the arrowroot dissolved in a little water.

   If the stock reduces too fast, top it up with a little more cold water. Skim the stock as it reduces and after you have added any more water.

To complete

6.   Season the rabbit with salt and pepper and fry in a hot pan with a little groundnut oil until sealed on each side. Remove the liver and kidneys which require no more cooking and place the rabbit cubes on butter paper or tin foil. Complete the cooking for 5 minutes in a hot oven, preheated to 400°F (200°C) Gas 6. Rabbit cooks quickly and will be very dry, like cottonwool, if overcooked.
7.   Pour the stock, mustard and cream into a small saucepan with any cooking juices from the rabbit. Bring this to the boil and then whisk in the olive oil and grated cheese.
8.   Spoon the sauce over the rabbit and serve with fresh pasta or mashed potatoes.

6

OFFAL, INCLUDING FOIE GRAS

Throughout history people have of necessity made use of every part of the animals they eat. Sensitivity almost amounting to a taboo exists over the consumption of certain parts and it is probably unwise to serve offal at a dinner party where you do not know all your guests. Liver is the most widely acceptable, ox tongue for sandwiches not far behind. Yet most people eat sausages and meat pies with no second thought.

This is a waste. The attraction of offal is not just in its very savoury and individual flavours but also the variety of texture on offer. Tripe, kidneys, sweetbreads and liver could not be more different to butcher's meat or each other, and hold out many more possibilities to an able cook than any piece of steak or chop.

Ironically, good liver and sweetbreads are extremely expensive. Traditional associations with poverty have sadly not affected the market price of these titbits, so somebody out there must be buying them up as well as myself.

We have all suffered from the fondness of institutions – schools, hospitals, prisons, depending on your experience – to serve poorly prepared and overcooked ox liver. Put these memories – along with detention and homework – out of your mind. Think rather of charcuteries, brasseries, succulent grilled calf's liver with some crisp rashers of bacon, and a glass of really good Burgundy. Inhibitions over offal are all in the mind, not in the mouth.

Purchase and preparation

The offal you buy should be young, fresh and pale. When buying sweetbreads look out for the ones that are thick, round and shaped like your fist. Calf's kidney and liver should be light in colour, almost tan, otherwise you will have to soak them in milk.

Lamb offal is cheaper and is second choice to calf's except of course when comparing top quality lamb's to lower quality veal.

As a general rule liver and kidneys should be cooked quickly, flash-fried or grilled to seal any juices and flavour, caramelising the outside and leaving the centre moist and tender.

Brains and sweetbreads need soaking for a couple of hours in cold water. Sweetbreads are excellent braised; their flavour becomes more delicate and savoury. The most usual treatment, though, is blanching – bringing to the boil in a pot of herbs, water and wine – followed by slicing and frying. Both are good.

With dressed tripe and pickled ox tongue you are rather at the mercy of your butcher. In Italy – Tuscany and Umbria especially – there are good tripe dishes to be had everywhere, but I have not managed to reproduce them properly at home. Perhaps it's how the tripe is dressed. I hope it isn't me.

Foie gras

Foie gras is almost a category on its own. I certainly never think of it in terms of liver. Goose foie gras is richer and more highly flavoured than duck foie gras. Contemporary taste leans towards the duck liver, and this is my preference also. Full of cholesterol, very rich, and a difficult dish to serve as a starter as it needs sweetish wines which are awkward to follow, it is nevertheless wonderful, one of life's treats.

CALF'S LIVER WITH WATERCRESS AND SHALLOT SAUCE

You will almost certainly buy the liver ready sliced by your butcher, but if you have any choice, and are buying top quality liver, have it sliced thicker than usual, say ⅓ in (8 mm) thick. The liver flavour will be more pronounced.

Check that the outer membrane has been removed, otherwise it will pull the liver out of shape as it cooks. The meat should be fresh and clean looking, with little smell. Only inferior liver needs soaking in milk to remove excess blood.

The liver cooks quickly and will be the last job on this dish; the potatoes that accompany it will take the longest. I think mashed potatoes are ideal with calf's liver, especially made with garlic-scented oil.

The potatoes

1.   It is best to cook the potatoes in their jackets, which retains the flavour, and to peel them after. Follow the instructions on page 112.
2.   Skin the potatoes, and add ½ teaspoon salt and several turns of the pepper mill. Mash the potatoes, and add the milk.
3.   Heat the olive oil with the garlic and then strain this on to the potatoes. Beat with a wooden spoon until light. Keep warm.

The sauce base

4.   In a small pan sweat the shallots with ½ oz (15 g) of the butter, then moisten with vermouth. Keep to one side.
5.   Pick over the watercress. You can use some stalks as well as leaves, but take care to remove any yellow leaves, anything that does not smell fresh and peppery, and the rougher, hairier parts of the stalk. Wash thoroughly, then chop the watercress, not too finely.

To complete

6.   Heat the pan well before cooking the liver so that it will seal instantly. Season the liver at the last moment with black pepper and salt – disregard any advice you may have heard about salting the liver after cooking instead of before. Brush with oil. Fry quickly – 30–45 seconds per side – and remove the liver from the pan. Keep warm.
7.   Combine the contents of the shallot pan and the watercress in the same pan with the liver juices and residue. Pour in the cream. Whisk in, piece by piece, the remaining softened butter until the sauce has thickened. This is best done off the heat so that the sauce does not split. Add the lemon juice and if it gets too thick let it down with a few more drops of vermouth.
8.   Put the mashed potato on to the plates, pour on the sauce, and place the liver on top.

Serves 4

4 × 5–6 oz (150–175 g) slices
   calf's liver
salt and freshly ground black
   pepper
groundnut oil

Potatoes
1½ lb (675 g) maincrop
   potatoes, scrubbed
1 fl oz (25 ml) milk
1 fl oz (25 ml) olive oil
2 garlic cloves, peeled and
   crushed

Sauce
4 oz (100 g) shallots, peeled and
   finely chopped
2 oz (50 g) unsalted butter
2 fl oz (50 ml) dry vermouth
1 bunch watercress
2 fl oz (50 ml) double cream
juice of ½ lemon

Calf's Sweetbreads with Caramelised Shallots and Balsamic Vinegar Sauce

This dish is made interesting by contrasts. It is, substantially, a sandwich of firmly braised sweetbread between crisp potato galettes. The flavours are a balance of balsamic vinegar, caramelised shallots, and good olive oil. No one flavour should predominate, and balsamic vinegar, especially a really good old one, will sharpen and enhance the delicate flavour of sweetbreads without upstaging it.

It is not difficult to make but I recommend that you make the stock a day or two in advance. Though it is not labour intensive, it takes time.

I have heard many wild and weird stories about what sweetbreads may be. They are in fact glands near the base of the throat, and they perform tasks a lot pleasanter than do the kidneys and liver. I cannot understand why anyone should be timid about eating them. This recipe is as good an introduction as any if you haven't cooked them before.

The veal stock

Serves 4

1½ lb (675 g) calf's sweetbreads
aromatics: slices of onion, leek and carrot, sprigs of thyme
salt and freshly ground black pepper
a dash of wine vinegar

Veal stock
1 lb (450 g) veal bones
1 each of the following: onion, leek, tomato, carrot, garlic clove, small sprig of thyme
4 fl oz (120 ml) red wine
1 teaspoon arrowroot

Potato galettes
1½ lb (675 g) potatoes
2 tablespoons groundnut oil

Caramelised shallots
12 shallots
groundnut oil
1 teaspoon sugar

To complete
2 tablespoons olive oil
2 tablespoons balsamic vinegar

1. Cut the bones into approximately 1 in (2.5 cm) pieces. Roast them in a preheated 400°F (200°C) Gas 6 oven, until they are golden brown, approximately 40 minutes. Try to avoid blackening them because this makes the stock bitter. Lift them from the roasting tray to a saucepan with a slotted spoon so that you take the minimum amount of grease. Empty the fat from the roasting tray into an old tin can rather than pouring it down the sink.

2. Pour 2 pints (1.2 litres) of water into the tray and boil hard for a minute. This process – deglazing – will capture all the flavour from the bone-roasting process. Pour this on to the bones in the pan.

3. Peel and roughly cube the vegetables and garlic, then fry them until they start to brown. Season with salt and pepper and the small sprig of thyme. Add the red wine and boil hard for a few seconds. Pour this mixture into the pan with the bones and water.

4. Bring the stock to the boil, and let it simmer for 2 hours, skimming carefully. Strain it into a smaller saucepan.

5. Add a further 10 fl oz (300 ml) of cold water, which will cause most of the imperfections in the stock to rise to the top where they can be skimmed off. Reduce by about half. You should have just over 10 fl oz (300 ml) of reduced veal stock.

6. Mix the arrowroot with a little water in a cup, and whisk it into the stock to thicken slightly. Strain the stock into a clean container and keep it until needed. (If not needed immediately, let it cool, and refrigerate.)

The sweetbreads

7.   Soak overnight in cold water.

8.   Carefully cut away most of the membrane from the outside, leaving just enough to hold the lobes together.

9.   Place in a saucepan with the aromatics, a little salt and black pepper, and a dash of wine vinegar. Add enough water to just cover the breads, then cover with a circle of buttered paper.

   Use your head when choosing a saucepan. If you use a huge one that needs gallons of water, you will overcook the breads by the time the water boils.

10.   Bring the pan to the boil, then take it from the heat immediately, and leave the sweetbreads to cool in the cooking liquor. They should then look set, but will be still soft, almost gelatinous to the touch.

The potato galettes

11.   Peel and wash the potatoes but don't leave them in the water. Grate through the coarsest setting of your grater, and season with salt and pepper.

12.   Make eight galettes each from a tablespoon of grated potato, about 3 in (7.5 cm) diameter and ¼ in (6 mm) thick. Fry them one at a time in the groundnut oil, until crisp on the outside with a soft interior.

The caramelised shallots

13.   Peel the shallots and fry them quickly in a little oil in a pan so that they are brown on the outside, about 3 or 4 minutes.

14.   Add the sugar and a little black pepper, then cook them in a hot oven – say, 400°F (200°C) Gas 6 – until they are soft, about 15–20 minutes.

To complete

15.   Slice the sweetbreads into escalopes about ⅓ in (8 mm) thick. Season with salt and pepper and brush with some of the olive oil.

16.   Re-boil the reduced veal stock with a tablespoon of the balsamic vinegar. Keep boiling until it reaches a shiny and slightly syrupy consistency.

17.   Quickly fry the sweetbreads in a red-hot, dry pan. They shouldn't take more than a minute on each side.

18.   Place one potato galette in the centre of each plate. Put a slice of sweetbread, or two if they are small, on each potato galette. Dribble over a little olive oil and balsamic vinegar, and place another potato galette on top.

19.   Pour some sauce around and put three caramelised shallots next to the sweetbreads.

CALF'S BRAINS IN BROWN BUTTER

A set of uncooked calf's brains does not look mouth-watering, in fact, a sight more reminiscent of Burke and Hare than anything gastronomic. Overcome this challenge, for the taste is delicate and savoury, and the texture pleasantly creamy.

Calf's brains used to be a staple brasserie dish, often served as part of a head meat collage – *tête de veau vinaigrette* – with herb and shallot dressing. Along with similar dishes, ox tongue, pigs' trotters, and tripe, they are very much part of another generation's eating habits, and now, like flowered shirts, it is their turn to come back into fashion.

You may have to wait for a while for well prepared *tête de veau* to be readily available (unless you have an exceptional butcher), but calf's brains are not too tricky, and they are inexpensive. Brains are the most delicately flavoured offal, and rich sauces are not appropriate.

The brains

1.   The best things in the world to eat, like brains and foie gras, require the most attention in basic preparation, or else they are very nasty. Soak the brains for 24 hours in several changes of cold water.
2.   They will be soft and you don't need anything other than your fingertips to clean them. Each brain will separate into larger pieces and a smaller piece which you should discard. Pinch away the creamy white parts from the underside of the brain, also any damaged or very dark areas.
3.   Put the brains into a saucepan with the white wine and shallot, squeezing in a little lemon juice and seasoning with salt and pepper. Add just enough water to cover them, then put a circle of buttered or greaseproof paper on top.
4.   Bring to the boil and remove from the heat. Allow them to cool in the cooking liquor.

Serves 4

2 sets calf's brains
2 fl oz (50 ml) white wine
1 shallot, peeled and sliced
1 lemon
salt and freshly ground pepper

To complete
8 oz (225 g) unsalted butter
1 teaspoon chopped parsley

To complete

5.   Remove the brains from the cooking liquor and pat dry. Season each with salt and pepper.
6.   Melt a knob of butter (say 2 oz/50 g) in a warm pan. When it is sizzling hot, but before it browns, add the brains. Fry until nicely coloured, almost crisped on each side, about 7 minutes a side.
    Once brains are blanched, you can't really hurt the texture by overcooking.
7.   Lift them from the pan on to warmed plates. Squeeze a little lemon juice on each one.

8. Heat the rest of the butter in the pan you have used to fry the brains. As it turns brown, strain it into a jug or container and add the chopped parsley. Pour this foaming brown butter over each brain.

If you pour the butter straight from the pan on to the plate, you will find the plate is showered with specks of butter; unfortunately it looks like you forgot to wash it.

BOILED OX TONGUE WITH BEETROOT

Ox tongue tastes better hot, but needs a sauce or relish. My preference is for a sharp vegetable accompaniment such as beetroot or celeriac, and maybe soft mashed potato, rather than the traditional Madeira sauce.

When choosing beetroot look for small, even-sized specimens. Cutting the vegetable will allow the colour to bleed away as it cooks.

Serves 4

1 × 2½ lb (1.1 kg) pickled ox tongue
2 lb (900 g) small beetroots, washed
salt and freshly ground black pepper
2 tablespoons white wine vinegar
2 tablespoons olive oil

To complete
a bunch of corn salad (*mâche*)

1. Soak the tongue overnight in cold water.
2. Drain, and place in a large pan. Cover with fresh water, and bring to the boil. There will be scum rising to the surface which you will need to skim off with a ladle.

Let the water barely simmer. The tongue will need about 2½–3 hours cooking.
3. After 1 hour add the beetroots. Depending on their size they will be ready in 1½–2 hours, the same time as the tongue.
4. Lift the beetroots from the water. Peel away the skin and chop the beetroots into small dice. Place in a bowl. Season with salt and pepper then dress with vinegar and olive oil. Keep warm.

To complete

5. Lift the tongue on to a cutting board. Peel off the skin and cut away any little bones, gristle or other debris. Slice the tongue, not too thinly.
6. Place a mound of the warm beetroot in the centre of the plate, and lay two slices of tongue against it. Garnish with the corn salad.

Terrine of Duck Foie Gras

Success in this dish is about careful preparation – the cooking is easy. It will concentrate the mind wonderfully if you keep the receipts for the ingredients in front of you as you work! Carelessness will come expensive.

1.   Cut each liver horizontally into three or four slices.
2.   Allow the slices to warm slowly to room temperature. These livers have a high fat content, and become very soft when not refrigerated.
3.   When soft, carefully pick out all nerves and veins, a messy job. Use your fingertips to lift up the veins from the liver. Don't forget to take off the outer membrane. This is a very important stage of the recipe – the more care you exercise in cleaning the liver the better the terrine will be.
4.   Season each slice liberally, on both sides, with salt, pepper and nutmeg.
5.   Arrange the slices in layers in a terrine. I use a Le Creuset one, measuring 12 × 3 in (30 × 7.5 cm). After each layer sprinkle with the port and Armagnac.

   Use decent port – a ten-year-old tawny is just fine. (Words like 'ruby' or 'vintage character' on the label often mean nasty and coarse, and represent a false economy when you consider the cost of the foie gras over which you are pouring it.)
6.   Refrigerate for 6–8 hours or overnight. The livers will have absorbed most of the port and brandy and will have become firm again.
7.   Place the terrine in a roasting dish half filled with cold water, and cook in the middle of a cool oven – 300°F (150°C) Gas 2 – for 20 minutes. It won't look cooked but it is. If you cook any longer you will end up with half the quantity of terrine and pints of butter-like fat.
8.   Lay a plastic card or a couple of spatulas along the top and then weight with three 2 oz (50 g) weights – remove them when the terrine is completely cold and set.
9.   Reduce the consommé by half with any juices from the terrine. Pour this over the terrine and chill to set. The reduced consommé will set to jelly, filling gaps in the terrine and making it easier to slice.
10.   Turn terrine out, or serve from the dish. Slice with a sharp, warm knife, and serve with brioche toast or potato bread (see page 114).

Serves 12

3 duck foie gras (about
    4 lb/1.8 kg in weight)
salt and freshly ground black
    pepper
freshly grated nutmeg
5 fl oz (150 ml) port
2½ fl oz (65 ml) Armagnac
10 fl oz (300 ml) chicken
    consommé (see page 119)

SAUTEED DUCK FOIE GRAS IN SALAD WITH WALNUT DRESSING

Here are three thoughts to help you succeed with the technique of sautéing foie gras. Foie gras, unsurprisingly, is very fat so pan-frying it requires the addition of no more. The livers must seal instantly otherwise they shrivel and shrink leaving you only rather expensive fatty blobs, so the pan must be very hot. Thirdly, sautéed foie gras is very rich so you won't need much; design a dish where a small amount of foie gras will be countered by a larger amount of other ingredients.

Serves 4

4 × 3 oz (75 g) slices duck foie gras
a selection of salad leaves: frisée, lollo rosso, cos lettuce and corn salad (*mâche*)
1 carrot
1 avocado
salt and freshly ground black pepper
4 tablespoons walnut oil
1 tablespoon sherry vinegar
1 tablespoon sherry

1. Check that the slices of foie gras have no nerve or membrane. If they do, then gently lift them out with your fingertips and return the liver to the refrigerator.
2. Wash and thoroughly dry the lettuces. Compose the leaves into four salads.
3. Peel and finely chop the carrot. Sprinkle this over the leaves. Peel the avocado and cut into strips. Add this also to the salads.
4. Salt the lettuces and dress them with 2 tablespoons of walnut oil and a few drops of sherry vinegar. This is easily done by drizzling the oil and vinegar over the salads with a pastry brush.
5. Heat a frying pan. Season the foie gras and quickly fry it on both sides. Lift out of the pan and on to kitchen paper.
6. Pour off most of the dark foie gras butter from the pan. Add sherry and sherry vinegar to deglaze. Add the remaining walnut oil and boil hard so that the dressing emulsifies. Strain into a saucepan.
7. Tuck the foie gras into each salad. Pour a band of warm dressing around each plate and serve quickly.

SAUTEED DUCK FOIE GRAS WITH SESAME

1. Season the slices of foie gras liberally with salt and pepper.
2. Heat a dry frying pan until it is red hot. Fry the liver on both sides. Lift the slices on to kitchen paper to drain.
3. Discard the foie gras fat in the frying pan and sauté the pine kernels, celery and tomato for a few seconds.
4. Spoon this garnish, with a pinch of five-spice powder and soy sauce, on to each plate. Sprinkle the foie gras with sesame seeds and place on top.

Serves 4

4 × 2 oz (50 g) slices duck foie gras
salt and freshly ground black pepper
1 tablespoon pine kernels
4 oz (100 g) celery, trimmed and chopped
4 firm tomatoes, skinned, de-seeded and chopped
1 pinch five-spice powder
1 dash soy sauce
1 oz (25 g) sesame seeds

7

DESSERTS AND FRUIT

After a large meal you may find your stamina failing at the pudding stage. A small helping of sorbet can freshen your appetite and allow you to embark on a more substantial dessert with some enthusiasm. This is the only point in a meal where a sorbet course is appropriate, never between fish and meat, for although a sorbet will undoubtedly wake up your tastebuds it also leaves a coating of sugar syrup across the palate which won't suit anything afterwards other than a dessert. Quite a few of the dishes which follow have an accompanying and sympathetic ice cream as an integral part. The reasoning here is the same.

Success with pastry-making comes with practice. Like many other disciplines, it takes some people longer than others to acquire a facility. Be patient, it is only a question of time and perseverance. Try to work with a light touch and remember to rest the pastry dough often. If you have over-handled it – which is the most common problem – it will need a little time to recover.

Fruit

As with vegetables, the range of fruit available year round has proliferated. Unfortunately, without the same degree of success. Rather bland exotica such as starfruit and paw paw are now permanently on offer along with oddly unsweet strawberries and dry peaches. Such are the lines of supply between Rungis, the Paris wholesale market, and our specialist dealers that imported fruit are supplanting local produce even when it is in season, and while Kent and Worcestershire are laden with plums my local shops are displaying only the Italian Santa Rosa. What a pity to miss out on such magnificent home-grown fruit; a ripe Marjorie's Seedling, the last plum to arrive, is every bit as luscious as any peach.

The era of permanent summer in the fruit market has definitely not yet arrived. Stick by what is in season.

Friandises/petits-fours

Almost nobody eats these little things and they involve such disproportionate hard work. I am constrained, by convention, to make an array of
chocolates, dipped fruit, marzipan and biscuits, but you are not.

In the baking chapter which follows there are recipes for biscuits such as
brandy snaps and pistachio tuiles which are more than adequate for the job.
Some fresh cherries steeped in brandy would also fit the bill and have the
bonus, if uneaten, of being a treat for the cook next day when all guests have
gone.

POPPYSEED PARFAIT WITH PLUM SAUCE

You don't need an ice-cream machine for this frozen dessert. The plums are stewed and then blended as sauce. I don't normally like to change a fruit's texture in a liquidiser, but stewed plums have a defeated look which is no loss.

The parfait

Serves 4

Parfait
4 egg yolks
4 oz (100 g) caster sugar
1 tablespoon honey
8 fl oz (250 ml) milk
1 vanilla pod
14 fl oz (400 ml) double cream
4 oz (100 g) poppyseeds

Plum sauce
1 lb (450 g) red plums
8 oz (225 g) granulated sugar
juice of ½ lemon

1. Make a sabayon with the egg yolks, sugar and honey. This entails whisking the ingredients together over a very low heat until the mixture cooks, first fluffing up and then thickening, without scrambling the egg.
2. Bring the milk and vanilla pod to the boil, then strain. Whisk the hot flavoured milk into the sabayon, then leave to cool.
3. Whip the cream and then fold it, with the poppyseeds, into the sabayon and milk mixture.
4. Spoon this into a dish – an oblong Pyrex dish is probably ideal. Freeze at least until frozen.

The plum sauce

5. Easy. Put the plums, sugar, lemon juice and 10 fl oz (300 ml) water into a saucepan. Bring to the boil, cover and simmer for 10 minutes. Pick out any stones and liquidise in a blender. Leave to cool.

To complete

6. Turn the parfait out of the dish. To do this, dip the dish base in warm water for a few seconds, then invert. Serve in slices, with a spoonful of plum sauce to the side.

RHUBARB SORBET

There are a few ground rules for success with sorbets, many of which apply to ice cream also.

Make and churn your sorbet as near as possible to when you wish to eat it. Superficially it may appear that frozen puddings of any sort are a useful standby, possible to prepare days in advance. Not so. They deteriorate fairly rapidly, and home-made ice creams are likely to give you stomach trouble if kept too long. Don't keep ice cream any longer in the freezer than you would keep custard in the fridge. Remember that commercial companies add preservatives and are geared up to thorough pasteurisation.

If you haven't got a machine, place the sorbet mixture in suitable containers, cover, and freeze until frozen but still soft. Remove from the freezer and container, and beat hard until smooth. Re-freeze, and repeat this process once more.

Serves 4

1 lb (450 g) rhubarb, trimmed
8 oz (225 g) granulated sugar
juice of ½ lemon

1. Dissolve the sugar in 10 fl oz (300 ml) water. Add the lemon juice, and bring this to the boil.
2. Chop the rhubarb, then cook it in the syrup until soft, about 10 minutes.
3. Blend to a pulp in a food processor or liquidiser. Allow to cool.
4. Churn for 10–15 minutes, or freeze and beat as above.
5. Serve in scoops, with brandy snaps (see page 109).

BRANDY AND WHITE WINE SORBET

Alcohol in sorbets acts as anti-freeze. A little will soften the texture of the sorbet; too much and it may not set. This one is good as a pudding, but it is also one of the few that can be served as a separate course.

Serves 4

1 fl oz (25 ml) brandy
10 fl oz (300 ml) white wine
10 oz (275 g) granulated sugar
juice of ½ lemon

1. Dissolve the sugar in 5 fl oz (150 ml) water. Bring to the boil and then cool.
2. Add the lemon juice, wine and brandy. Mix it well and then test the flavour by drinking a teaspoonful. If it doesn't taste delicious at this stage something is wrong. The acidity and body of the wine will affect the balance so you may need to make adjustments such as adding a little more lemon.
3. Churn or freeze. This will take longer than a fruit sorbet, probably 20 minutes. This sorbet, like some persons, has more alcohol than is good for it and takes time to set. Don't expect it to reach the level of firmness of something like a lemon sorbet. It is, at its best, slightly slushy.
4. Serve in chilled glasses.

RED FRUIT SALAD WITH VANILLA ICE CREAM

Sadly there will only ever be two or three weeks a year when this salad can be made, that brief period when strawberries have not quite finished but raspberries have begun.

The vanilla ice cream

Serves 4

Vanilla ice cream
8 egg yolks
3 oz (75 g) caster sugar
10 fl oz (300 ml) double cream
10 fl oz (300 ml) milk
1 whole vanilla pod

Fruit salad
8 oz (225 g) fresh cherries,
   pitted
1 punnet ripe strawberries
1 punnet ripe raspberries
½ punnet redcurrants
1 punnet tayberries
3 oz (75 g) caster sugar
juice of 1 lemon
1 tablespoon cognac

1.   Beat the egg yolks and sugar together until they are creamy and thick. Boil the cream and milk with the vanilla pod, then pour into a blender and process.
2.   Pour on to the egg and sugar whisking all the time. Stir over a low heat until the texture first loosens and then thickens slightly, showing it has cooked.
3.   Leave the custard to cool completely, then churn in an ice-cream maker. If you have no such machine, place the custard in the deep freeze and stir it at half-hourly intervals until set.

The fruit salad

4.   Clean all the fruit.
5.   Bring the cherries, sugar and lemon juice to the boil then allow to cool.
6.   Add cognac and all the other fruit. Leave to macerate in the refrigerator for at least an hour.

To complete

7.   The salad will have produced its own syrup. Spoon it into soup bowls and place a scoop of ice cream on top. Don't be worried by black flecks in the ice cream, these are particles of vanilla pod and taste delicious.

CARAMEL AND APPLE TART WITH CARAMEL ICE CREAM

Caramel and apples is not a new combination. People have enjoyed eating them together from whenever toffee apples were dreamed up. This is my variation on that theme and it works well.

The choice of apple is important. Cooking apples such as Bramleys are quite useless, too sour and inclined to disintegrate. A sharp but well-flavoured dessert apple such as a Granny Smith is fine. I don't use Cox's Orange Pippin for cooking though they are great for eating if they are ripe. We have planted both of these classic varieties in our orchard at Gidleigh Park.

The ice cream contrasts nicely with the warm tart and caramel. If you have neither the time nor inclination to make it, use a spoonful of Mrs Hurdle's Jersey cream (or the best clotted cream you can get if you don't live in Central Devon) instead.

Don't use ready-made pastry from a shop. It will give an unpleasant greasy aftertaste and spoil the dish.

The caramel ice cream

1. Dissolve the sugar in a little water, and boil hard until it caramelises. It will turn a light brown colour, just past golden yellow. Take the pan off the heat at this point and let it develop into a rich brown colour as it cools slightly.
2. Pour on the milk and cream. Whisk all this on to the egg yolks in a pan.
3. Stir over a low heat until the mixture thickens slightly, giving the consistency of thin custard. Allow this to cool, then freeze, preferably in an ice-cream machine.

The sweet pastry

4. Sieve the flour and sugar together into a bowl.
5. Rub in the butter and egg with your fingertips until the consistency of fine breadcrumbs. Form into a ball, cover with cling film, and rest in a cool place for an hour.
6. Roll out on a floured board to ⅛ in (3 mm) thickness. Line four tart cases of 4 in (10 cm) in diameter. Rest them again for an hour, again in a cool place.
7. Put aluminium foil and beans into each tart case and then bake blind at 350°F (180°C) Gas 4, for 10 minutes.

To complete

The object is a warm tart and warm sauce with the cold ice cream. The quicker you work, the warmer it will be.
8. Peel, core, slice and cook two of the apples in a covered saucepan with

Serves 4

6 apples

Caramel ice cream
8 oz (225 g) granulated sugar
10 fl oz (300 ml) milk
10 fl oz (300 ml) double cream
8 egg yolks

Sweet pastry
8 oz (225 g) plain flour
2 oz (50 g) caster sugar
5 oz (150 g) unsalted butter
1 egg

Caramel sauce
6 oz (175 g) unsalted butter
9 oz (250 g) granulated sugar
1 fl oz (25 ml) Calvados
5 fl oz (150 ml) double cream

1 tablespoon water until they start to disintegrate, about 2 or 3 minutes, then purée. Spoon this purée into the tart cases.

9. Make the caramel sauce by cooking the butter and sugar, preferably in a copper pan (which spreads the heat most evenly), until it caramelises, i.e. turns a rich brown colour. Add the Calvados and cream, and stir to blend off the heat. Take care because the caramel will spit.

10. Peel and core the remaining apples. Poach for 2 minutes in enough water to cover, then slice them thinly and fan them across the purée in each tart.

11. Place a tart on each plate. Coat with caramel sauce, and serve with a scoop of caramel ice cream.

CHERRY BAKEWELL TART

Bakewell tart is evidently known as Bakewell pudding in Bakewell, though that's not particularly important unless you are preparing for *Mastermind*.

Cherries and apricots complement the almond flavour really well. If I use cherries – we are talking about fresh cherries here – I like them to cook in the tart, their juice colouring and flavouring the frangipane. If I use apricots I cook them separately and sieve them, serving them like a warm jam next to a slice of tart, and with clotted cream.

The pastry is awkward and has a tendency to come apart when uncooked. It is worth the effort, though, for its taste is part of the tart's flavour and not just an edible casing.

The pastry

Serves 4

Pastry
8 oz (225 g) plain flour
3 oz (75 g) ground almonds
4 oz (100 g) caster sugar
6 oz (175 g) unsalted butter, soft but not melted
2 egg yolks
½ teaspoon vanilla essence

Cherry frangipane
8 oz (225 g) unsalted butter
8 oz (225 g) caster sugar
4 eggs, beaten
8 oz (225 g) ground almonds
8 oz (225 g) fresh cherries, stoned

1. Sieve together all the dry ingredients.
2. With the fingertips rub in the butter, egg yolks and vanilla essence to form a dough. Rest the dough in the fridge for at least 1 hour.
3. Roll out on floured cling film to ⅛ in (3 mm) thickness.
4. Turn the pastry (which is very short and difficult to handle) on to a deep 10 in (25 cm) tart case, and remove the cling film.
5. Bake blind (i.e. without filling, using a layer of foil and beans to weight the pastry) for 15 minutes at 350°F (180°C), Gas 4.

The cherry frangipane

6. Cream the butter and sugar together.
7. Slowly beat in the eggs.
8. Fold in the ground almonds.

To complete

9. Scatter the cherries on the pastry case, and spoon the frangipane filling on top.
10. Bake for 30 minutes at 350°F (180°C) Gas 4.

CHOCOLATE MILLE-FEUILLES

Substituting cocoa powder for a little of the flour in puff pastry will produce crisp chocolate mille-feuilles. The flavour, though distinct, is delicate, so avoid cluttering the dish with colourful fruit; even the usually compatible orange or cherries will upstage the pastry. A few toasted almond flakes or hazelnuts would be all right but best of all is to explore a chocolate theme throughout and serve the pastry, still warm, with cocoa pastry cream filling and a few shavings of dark chocolate for decoration.

If you have made puff pastry before, this variation is simple. If you have not, then remember to rest the pastry well every time you roll it.

This pastry recipe makes more than you need to serve four – unless you are very hungry – but it freezes beautifully. Divide the pastry in half and use one part only for the mille-feuilles.

The puff pastry

Serves 4

Puff pastry
1 lb (450 g) strong flour
1½ oz (40 g) cocoa powder
1 oz (25 g) icing sugar
1 lb (450 g) unsalted butter
a pinch of salt

Pastry cream
4 egg yolks
4 oz (100 g) caster sugar
1 oz (25 g) cocoa powder
2 oz (50 g) plain flour
1 pint (600 ml) milk

To complete
4 fl oz (120 ml) double cream
4 oz (100 g) dark chocolate

1.   Sieve the flour, cocoa powder and icing sugar together. Melt 2 oz (50 g) of the butter, and add this, 8 fl oz (250 ml) water and a pinch of salt to the flour. Knead this into a smooth, firm paste and rest it in the fridge for half an hour.
2.   Roll out the paste into a square about ¾ in (2 cm) thick. Flatten the remaining butter – I do this by sandwiching the butter between its own wrapping papers, and then flattening it with a rolling pin. Place the flattened butter in the centre of the paste and fold the edges of the square over so it is completely covered.
3.   Roll the paste into a long rectangle ¾ in (2 cm) thick, and then fold the two ends to meet at the centre. Again fold the two ends to meet in the middle. Leave this to rest in the fridge for 30 minutes.
4.   This rolling and folding process is known as a double turn. You will need to repeat this *three* times, giving four double turns in total. Take care to rest the pastry well between each.
5.   Divide in two, and store one-half in the fridge (or freezer) for another day. Roll out the pastry as thinly as possible. Put the pastry on to a baking tray and prick the surface all over with a fork. Rest this in the fridge for 30 minutes.
6.   Bake in a hot oven, preheated to 400°F (200°C) Gas 6, for 10 minutes until crisp. Cut the pastry into 2½ in (6 cm) squares. You are going to build them into mille-feuilles so they should be exactly the same size and shape.

The pastry cream

7.   Whisk the egg yolks and sugar together until they are white. Stir in the cocoa powder and flour. Bring the milk to the boil and whisk on to the other

ingredients. Strain back into the saucepan and bring to the boil, stirring. Pour into a bowl to cool. If you sprinkle a little sugar over the surface, no skin will form.

To complete

8. Whisk the cream and fold it into the chocolate custard. Put a tablespoonful of this on to a puff pastry square and top with another square. In this way build up each of the mille-feuilles so that there are four layers of chocolate puff pastry sandwiching the pastry cream. Grate some dark chocolate to decorate the plate.

STEAMED ORANGE PUDDING

Steamed puddings are hefty eating. Plan a light main course to precede one. If orange isn't what you fancy, lemon will stand in adequately – or whatever flavour you want!

Serves 4

4 oz (100 g) unsalted butter
4 oz (100 g) caster sugar
4 oz (100 g) self-raising flour
1 oz (25 g) fresh breadcrumbs
½ teaspoon baking powder
2 eggs
2 tablespoons milk
juice and zest of 2 oranges
4 tablespoons golden syrup

1. Cream the butter and sugar together.
2. Stir in the dry ingredients.
3. Beat in the eggs, then add the milk and orange juice and zest.
4. Butter the sides of four small bowls or four large ramekin dishes. Put a tablespoon of syrup in each bowl and pour on the batter. Fasten silver foil loosely across the tops to act as lids, and tie on with string.
5. Place the bowls or ramekins in a roasting tray half-filled with boiling water. Either steam on top of the stove for 40 minutes, or start off on top, and then transfer when bubbling to an oven preheated to 300°F (150°C) Gas 2, and cook for the 40 minutes, until done.
6. Turn out of the bowls or dishes, and serve with clotted cream.

Warm Blackberry Soufflé with Almond Ice Cream

Soufflés are generally disappointing desserts. There is an element of theatre when one appears with its head standing high over the dish, and the punters assume that it took great skill to produce – the higher it stands, the cleverer the cook.

This is not so. The more egg you use, the higher and swifter it will rise. Also, the more egg you use, the more it will eat like a stringy omelette and leave you with a metallic, fried egg aftertaste.

The egg *should* be a vehicle for lightening and aerating the fruit or chocolate, and should be barely perceptible as a taste. Use ingredients like lemon or passionfruit with sharp distinct flavours. The flavour of whatever you use will be delicate after increasing the volume tenfold by whisked egg whites, so steer clear of anything bland. The distinctive flavour of blackberries tastes just fine.

The almond ice cream

1. Mix the milk and cream and then heat almost to boiling point with the ground almonds.
2. Toast the whole bleached almonds under a grill until brown, and then break them up into small granules in a food processor.
3. Whisk the egg yolks and sugar together. Then pour on the hot milk and cream mixture.
4. Whisk over a low heat until the mixture starts to thicken, then strain into a container and leave to cool.
5. Stir in the almond granules and freeze, preferably in an ice-cream machine.

The sauce

6. Pick over the blackberries to make sure none is mouldy. Remove a few nice ones to garnish the completed dish.
7. Squeeze the lemons. Combine the juice in a pan with the sugar and 10 fl oz (300 ml) of water, then boil with the fruit until it becomes a purée. Sieve into a container.

The soufflé-base mixture

8. Whisk two of the egg yolks with the sugar until they become white. Stir in the flour and then carefully whisk in the hot milk.

Serves 4

Almond ice cream
5 fl oz (150 ml) milk
5 fl oz (150 ml) double cream
1 oz (25 g) ground almonds
2 oz (50 g) whole bleached
  almonds
3 egg yolks
3 oz (75 g) caster sugar

Sauce
2 punnets blackberries
2 lemons
2 oz (50 g) granulated sugar

Soufflé-base mixture
6 egg yolks
2 oz (50 g) caster sugar
1 oz (25 g) plain flour
10 fl oz (300 ml) hot milk
4 egg whites

9.   Bring this mixture to the boil, stirring all the time, until it is the consistency of thick custard. Pour into a container until you are ready to complete the dish.

To make the soufflés

10.   Combine the soufflé-base mixture with half the sauce.
11.   Add and stir in the four remaining egg yolks.
12.   Whisk the egg whites until stiff, and fold them into the mixture.
13.   Butter four 10 fl oz (300 ml) soufflé dishes and spoon in the mixture.
14.   Bake in a moderately hot oven – 400°F (200°C) Gas 6 – for about 10 minutes. They should have risen well above the rim of the dishes.

To complete

15.   Spoon the remainder of the sauce on to the four plates. Decorate with the reserved blackberries.
16.   Carefully spoon the ice cream on to the sauce. Use two spoons that have been in warm water to shape and portion the ice cream.
17.   Finally, place the soufflés in their ramekins on to the plates and serve as soon as possible.

8

BAKING

Devon people eat good bread, and most towns still have a decent family-run bakery. Although you will rarely see sour dough or soda bread, you can expect reliable granary and half a dozen shapes of good white bread.

Sadly these shops double up as *pâtisseries*, a craft for which they are usually unsuited. Most windows have the same dismal selection of iced buns and doughnuts. Bakeries with notions of grandeur will pipe cream into these and feel they have catered to the fancy end of the market. What a turning point it will be when the cream money is spent on, say, better jam for the doughnut and better oil to cook it in.

In my own kitchen each new recruit starts by learning basic baking skills. It is as much the heart of cookery as good stocks. In restaurants people munch bread as they wait for their first courses. Palates are sharpest when stimulated by hunger; the smell of yeast, the crunch of crisp crust and the still warm taste of freshly baked bread convinces the punters that what is to follow will be good.

You need good flour to make good bread. It's okay to buy standard strong flour and dried yeast from the supermarket – you will still get a fresh, yeasty smelling product. But buy better flour from a specialist miller, and fresh yeast, and you are on the way to producing something really superior.

The breads I make, and describe in this chapter, aren't particularly difficult. My mother-in-law, a farmer's wife from southern Finland, makes better and more complex breads – wonderful rye and crispbreads especially. If the ease of my bread-making kindles an interest, then move on to books like Elizabeth David's *English Bread and Yeast Cookery*.

Biscuits

Biscuit-making is almost embarrassingly easy. There are a couple of rules, though, to which you should adhere. Biscuit doughs need to be cooled thoroughly and well rested before baking. Secondly, biscuits don't keep as well as you might imagine, even in lidded containers. Try to serve them fairly soon after baking, especially chocolate biscuits. It's easy to cook off just half a batch and leave the remainder of the dough in the fridge for another day.

GRANARY BREAD

If you are a novice bread-maker, I would begin with a brown bread. It is less temperamental, more sympathetic to inexperience. Don't worry if your dough doesn't rise as quickly as expected. Be patient for an hour, perhaps the room is colder than you thought.

Granary flour makes better bread than rolls. Shape the dough into baguettes for a crisp crust and soft inside, a bread that will still look attractive, served warm, with a meal.

Presumably you may substitute dried yeast for fresh if you follow the instructions on the packet, although I have never produced as good bread with it. Use an organically grown flour, it tastes better. And lastly, ignore any additives or enhancers you may find. I have never needed vitamin C to make dough rise. Neither will you.

This recipe makes a batch of ten small loaves, each one enough for a good portion. Should you need less, the remainder freezes very well.

Makes 10 small loaves

1 tablespoon honey
1¼ pints (750 ml) milk
2 oz (50 g) fresh yeast
3 lb (1.3 kg) granary flour
3 eggs
1 level tablespoon salt
6 oz (175 g) unsalted butter, melted

1.   Dissolve the honey in 5 fl oz (150 ml) of the milk, heated to lukewarm. Add the yeast and mix thoroughly. Leave this to stand in a warm place for 15 minutes by which time it should start to bubble.

2.   Mix the flour, eggs, salt and melted butter together in a large bowl. Add the yeasty milk and the remaining milk, and mix to a dough.

3.   Knead the dough for 10 minutes, then leave to prove until double in size. This will probably take an hour but could take only 30 minutes on a summer's day or 2 hours on a cold winter's evening. The dough should be covered with cling film.

4.   Preheat the oven to 450°F (230°C) Gas 8. Knock back the dough by lifting from the bowl and kneading for a few seconds. Shape into cigar-like loaves 9 × 2 in (23 × 5 cm).

5.   Lay these loaves on a greased baking tray and leave to prove, covered loosely with cling film again. When they have doubled in volume they are ready to bake. This should take 30 minutes.

6.   Bake the loaves in the preheated oven for about 20 minutes or until brown. Take the loaves off the trays or the bases will continue to cook and become hard.

WALNUT BREAD

A variety of granary bread, flavoured by rosemary and browned butter as well as walnuts. This bread suits both creamy and blue cheese. As with most breads it freezes well.

1.   Warm 2 tablespoons of water to blood temperature – just past lukewarm – and mix the yeast and salt into it. Leave in the warm to froth.

Makes about 6 small loaves

½ oz (15 g) fresh yeast
a pinch of salt
2 oz (50 g) unsalted butter
1 sprig fresh rosemary
2 oz (50 g) brown sugar
8 fl oz (250 ml) milk, warmed
1 lb (450 g) granary flour
2 oz (50 g) walnuts

2.   Heat the butter in a small pan with the rosemary until the butter starts to brown. Add the sugar and then the warmed milk.
3.   When this has cooled to lukewarm, strain on to the yeast in a large bowl, and add the granary flour. Mix to a dough.
4.   Roughly chop the walnuts and add them to the dough, kneading to incorporate.
5.   Cover the dough with a clean cloth or sheet of cling film and leave in a warm, draught-free spot to prove.
6.   When the dough has roughly doubled in bulk, perhaps an hour or two, knock it back, i.e. knead it a couple of times to deflate it.
7.   Shape into small baguettes and place on an oiled baking sheet. Leave to prove once more. When the loaves have doubled in volume, after about another 30 minutes, bake in an oven preheated to 400°F (200°C) Gas 6 for 15 minutes. They should be well browned, sound rather hollow when tapped and feel light when lifted.

As with most baking you may complete every step up to the second proving (step 7) quite well in advance and leave the bread in a fridge, covered with a cloth or cling film, until you want to bake it.

HAZELNUT AND APRICOT BREAD

This bread is good on its own, as a tea bread or with cheese. It is a white flour and yeast dough rolled in rye flour for extra flavour. Very simple and quick to make.

Makes 2 loaves

½ oz (15 g) fresh yeast
5 fl oz (150 ml) skimmed milk
1 teaspoon honey
2 oz (50 g) hazelnuts
4 oz (100 g) dried apricots
1 lb (450 g) strong white flour
1 teaspoon salt
1 fl oz (25 ml) nut oil, preferably hazelnut
2 oz (50 g) rye flour

1.   Mix the yeast with a tablespoonful of lukewarm skimmed milk and the teaspoonful of honey. Leave this somewhere warm for 10 minutes to froth.
2.   Chop the hazelnuts and apricots fairly roughly. You want to see and taste both in the finished loaf, but you won't want to break a tooth on an unexpected whole hazelnut.
3.   Mix the white flour, apricots, hazelnuts and salt in a large bowl.
4.   Add the oil, remaining milk and 5 fl oz (150 ml) water to the yeast. Mix these together and pour them on to the dry ingredients in the bowl.
5.   Knead to a firm dough. Cover with cling film and leave in a warm place until the dough has doubled in volume, probably about an hour.
6.   Knock back the dough by kneading it again for a few seconds. Divide the dough into two and roll each half in rye flour.
7.   Put the dough into two greased 1 lb (450 g) loaf tins, cover with cling film and leave in a warm place to prove a second time. When the dough has doubled in bulk (this will probably take less time than the first proving), the bread is ready to bake.
8.   Preheat the oven to 425°F (220°C) Gas 7. Bake the two loaves for 35–40 minutes. Remove from tins, and cool on wire racks.

SODA BREAD

Common all over Ireland, soda bread used to be cooked in lidded iron pots called bastables that were suspended over the fireplace.

This and potato bread remind me of childhood visits to my grandmother who lived in a small cottage by Lough Neigh. At that time the cottage had neither mains water nor electricity. It was a scenic spot next to an old churchyard overlooking the lakeshore. It cures me of nostalgia for anything other than lost innocence to remember how uncomfortable it must have been for her, and how few are the attractions of an outside lavatory and no bathroom.

Soda bread doesn't keep well. If you bake in the morning for the same evening, wrap the loaf in a clean cloth to prevent drying.

If you cannot find buttermilk, use skimmed milk or even half milk, half water, but you will need to double the quantity of cream of tartar.

I have seen recipes for soda bread using wholemeal flour or part wholemeal. I'm sure this would taste fine though I have never used it myself.

Makes 1 loaf

1 lb (450 g) plain flour
½ teaspoon cream of tartar
1 teaspoon bicarbonate of soda
1 teaspoon salt
15 fl oz (450 ml) buttermilk

1. Mix the flour, cream of tartar, bicarbonate of soda and salt.
2. Mix to a soft dough with the buttermilk.
3. Pat into a flattish round loaf and place on a greased baking sheet. Mark the loaf into quarters with a knife.
4. Bake for 45 minutes at 350°F (180°C) Gas 4.
5. Remove loaf from oven and place on a wire rack. Eat fairly swiftly while it's nice and warm.

BUTTERMILK ROLLS

Buttermilk is the slightly sharp, fatless by-product of butter-making, and is easy to obtain in a dairy-farming region like Devon. It may prove more difficult elsewhere. The substitution of skimmed milk and cream of tartar will also produce excellent rolls.

This recipe should produce between 15 and 20 rolls, depending on size. They are crisp, almost biscuit-like on the outside but soft and light inside. Just right for mopping up sauce.

Makes 20 rolls

1 oz (25 g) fresh yeast
15 fl oz (450 ml) buttermilk or
    15 fl oz (450 ml) skimmed
    milk and 1 teaspoon cream
    of tartar
1 teaspoon honey
1 lb 10 oz (750 g) strong white
    flour
1 teaspoon bicarbonate of soda
1 teaspoon salt
3 oz (75 g) unsalted butter,
    melted

1. Dissolve the yeast in a little buttermilk with the honey. Leave in a warm part of the kitchen for half an hour until it begins to froth.
2. Mix all the dry ingredients together, then add the buttermilk, the buttermilk yeast mixture, and half the melted butter. Make this into a dough and knead for 5 minutes.
3. Cover with a damp cloth or cling film and leave in a warm, draught-free place for an hour to rise.
4. Knock back the dough, kneading it for a few seconds so that it collapses back to its original volume. Divide the dough into two pieces. Roll out until

about ⅛ in (3 mm) thick. Brush both pieces with the rest of the melted butter.

5.　Now cut the dough into strips 2 in (5 cm) wide, and lay these strips on top of each other, about five strips high. Cut them into squares of about 2 in (5 cm). Pinch one corner of each square to seal the layers.

6.　Stand the squares, sealed edge downwards, in buttered Yorkshire pudding tins. Cover and leave them to rise for 1 hour.

7.　Bake in a hot oven – 425°F (220°C) Gas 7 – for about 15 minutes, until golden brown. Serve hot.

SESAME AND ROQUEFORT BISCUITS

These little biscuits, served hot from the oven, are regular offerings with drinks at Gidleigh Park. They are popular to an extent well beyond their simplicity to make. Only disadvantage – they leave a lot of crumbs to vacuum. Stilton or any other fine blue cheese can substitute for Roquefort.

Makes about 20 biscuits

4 oz (100 g) self-raising flour
4 oz (100 g) unsalted butter
4 oz (100 g) Roquefort cheese
2 oz (50 g) sesame seeds

1.　Rub the flour and butter together to crumbs.
2.　Crumble the cheese finely and add it to the mix.
3.　Rest the mixture well, at least 2 hours, in the fridge.
4.　Roll out to ¼ in (6 mm) thickness, and cut into whatever shapes you want. I roll them into small balls, 1 in (2.5 cm) in diameter.
5.　Roll them in or sprinkle them with sesame seeds and bake in a hot oven – 450°F (230°C) Gas 8 – until brown. This should take 10 minutes. Cool on wire racks.

SPICE CAKE

A dense, strongly flavoured fruitcake to eat with tea or coffee.

1 lb (450 g) honey
9 oz (250 g) granulated sugar
¼ teaspoon salt
1 tablespoon bicarbonate of
　soda
1 lb (450 g) wholemeal flour
3 oz (75 g) ground almonds
2 fl oz (50 ml) rum
4 teaspoons ground anise
½ teaspoon each of ground
　cinnamon, ground cloves and
　ground mace
8 oz (225 g) sultanas

1.　Blend the honey, sugar and 6 fl oz (175 ml) boiling water. Stir until all the sugar has dissolved.
2.　Stir in the salt, bicarbonate of soda and flour, a little at a time. Beat this together, preferably in an electric mixer, for 5 minutes.
3.　Beat in all the other ingredients.
4.　Spoon the mixture into a buttered 2 lb (900 g) loaf tin. The tin should be about two-thirds full. The batter will rise to fill the tin as it cooks.
5.　Bake in the middle of an oven, preheated to 325°F (160°C) Gas 3 for 1¼ hours. Try to avoid opening the oven door during the first 45 minutes of cooking. If the top of the cake becomes too dark you may cover it with silver foil or greaseproof paper.
6.　When cooked, let the spice cake cool in its tin for 10–15 minutes, then unmould on to a wire rack.
7.　When cool, wrap in cling film and store in the refrigerator. It will keep for weeks, the flavour improving and developing.

CHOCOLATE FUDGE CAKE

Cake made with breadcrumbs rather than flour might seem odd, but doesn't taste it. This is a cake for morning coffee or afternoon tea in smallish slices rather than a dessert.

The fudge cake

1. Melt the chocolate. There is no way to do this quickly. Break the chocolate into small pieces, place them in a bowl and stand the bowl in a pan of warm water. Alternatively leave the chocolate somewhere warm in the kitchen and be patient.
2. Cream the butter and caster sugar together until pale.
3. Add the eggs, beating them in one by one. If you have a mixing machine use it. Only when one egg is incorporated, add the next.
4. Mix the melted chocolate with the creamed eggs, butter and sugar. Add the vanilla then stir in the almonds and breadcrumbs.
5. Bake in a deep 10 in (25 cm) sponge tin for 45 minutes in a low oven – 325°F (160°C) Gas 3. Turn out of the tin straightaway and leave to cool.

1 lb (450 g) dark chocolate
1 lb (450 g) unsalted butter
1½ lb (675 g) caster sugar
12 eggs
2 drops vanilla essence
8 oz (225 g) ground almonds
10 oz (275 g) fresh white
  breadcrumbs

Icing
4½ oz (120 g) unsalted butter
3 oz (75 g) cocoa powder
9 oz (250 g) icing sugar

The icing

6. Melt the butter and then stir in the cocoa powder and icing sugar. Beat until smooth.
7. Spread the chocolate icing over the cold cake with a palette knife. Leave for 30 minutes to set properly in the fridge.

PISTACHIO TUILES

Tuiles are a fairly standard accompaniment to sorbet. The name comes from the saddle-like shape which is reminiscent of roof tiles in southern France. This Italian variation is also quite effective as a petit four.

1. Lightly whisk the egg whites to loosen the texture.
2. Whisk in the sugar, then mix in the melted butter followed by the flour.
3. Oil a baking sheet and put a teaspoonful of the mixture on to it. Use the back of a fork to spread the mixture into a circle.
4. Sprinkle some chopped pistachio nuts on top. Repeat until the mixture is used up. If your baking sheet isn't large enough you can, of course, cook the tuiles in relays.
5. Bake for about 6 minutes at 375°F (190°C) Gas 5. They should be a pale golden brown.

Makes 20 tuiles

4 egg whites
8 oz (225 g) caster sugar
4 oz (100 g) unsalted butter,
  melted
4 oz (100 g) plain flour
2 oz (50 g) pistachio nuts, peeled
  and roughly chopped

6.   Remove the tray from the oven. Lift off the biscuits with a palette knife. They are very soft and pliable at this stage. Lay each biscuit over a rolling pin so that they set in the classic curved shape.

BRANDY SNAPS

You may mould these crisp biscuits easily to any shape you fancy, or any size – a teaspoonful is good for petits fours. A 6 in (15 cm) biscuit cooled over an upturned sugar bowl will provide a container for syllabub or sorbet, and convert a scoop of ice cream into a creditable dessert.

Makes 20–100 depending on size

4 oz (100 g) granulated sugar
4 oz (100 g) unsalted butter
4 oz (100 g) golden syrup
4 oz (100 g) plain flour
¼ oz (7.5 g) ground ginger
juice of ½ lemon
1 tablespoon brandy

1.   Melt the sugar, butter and syrup together.
2.   Warm the flour. Add this, the ginger, lemon juice and brandy, to the melted butter, and mix together.
3.   Spoon the mixture, 6 in (15 cm) apart, on to a greased baking tray, and bake for 10 minutes at 350°F (180°C) Gas 4 until brown.
4.   As they cool, lift the biscuits with a palette knife on to a rolling pin so that they set in an attractive and fairly uniform shape.

MORNING BISCUITS

Baking these thin, crisp, almond biscuits is the kitchen's first job each day at Gidleigh Park. They are served warm with morning tea or coffee. We make the dough last thing at night. By morning it is rested perfectly.

Makes about 20 biscuits

2½ oz (65 g) whole almonds
10 oz (275 g) hard unsalted butter
9 oz (250 g) plain flour
3½ oz (90 g) caster sugar
a pinch of salt
1 large egg white
a few drops of vanilla essence

1.   Brown the almonds in the oven. Use a dry baking tray and a hot oven – 400°F (200°C) Gas 6. Shake the tray occasionally so that the almonds brown evenly. This should take 5 minutes only.
2.   Allow the almonds to cool and then grind in a food processor.
3.   Add the hard butter, piece by piece, then add the flour, sugar and salt. Process together.
4.   Add the egg white and vanilla essence, process briefly, then chill well for a minimum of 1 hour.
5.   Roll out the paste to ⅛ in (3 mm) thickness. Cut into 2 in (5 cm) rounds and then bake in a moderate oven – 325°F (160°C) Gas 3 – until brown, about 10 minutes.
   As the biscuits are thin they are liable to cook unevenly if your oven is small or even a little faulty. Watch them occasionally as they bake and, if necessary, turn the tray around.
6.   Move from baking tray to wire rack with a palette knife, and leave until cold.

SYRUP AND OATMEAL BISCUITS

I'm not an enormous fan of oatmeal. It tastes too much as if it's good for you. These biscuits are an exception.

1. Beat the butter and sugar together until white and creamy.
2. Stir in all the dry ingredients.
3. Stir in the golden syrup and 1 tablespoon hot water.
4. You will have a firm paste. Divide it into 20 small pieces. Rub each piece between the palms of your hands to form a ball. At this stage you may keep them in the fridge until you want to bake them. As with most biscuits they are better just out of the oven.
5. Place the biscuit paste balls at 2 in (5 cm) intervals on a greased baking tray. Bake for 15 minutes at 300°F (150°C) Gas 2. Cool on a wire rack.

Makes 20 biscuits

8 oz (225 g) unsalted butter
8 oz (225 g) caster sugar
8 oz (225 g) plain flour
8 oz (225 g) porridge oats
1 teaspoon baking powder
1 teaspoon bicarbonate of soda
2 tablespoons golden syrup

SHORTBREAD BISCUITS

This recipe makes good biscuits. You might prefer to make a thinner version with the same dough. This would be more crisp but taste less buttery.

1. Cream the butter and sugar together until light and fluffy.
2. Sift the flour and cornflour together and mix into the butter and sugar.
3. Form this paste into a ball, wrap in cling film and refrigerate for 1 hour.
4. Preheat the oven to 275°F (140°C) Gas 1.
5. Roll the paste out to a thickness of ⅓ in (8 mm). Cut into shapes and place on an oiled baking sheet. Refrigerate for 2 hours.
6. Bake for 25 minutes by which time the biscuits should be a pale golden colour.
7. Remove from the oven. Sprinkle with a little sugar and cool on wire racks.

Makes 25 biscuits

12 oz (350 g) unsalted butter
8 oz (225 g) caster sugar
14 oz (400 g) plain flour
4 oz (100 g) cornflour

CHOCOLATE CHUNK COOKIES

These American style cookies are best eaten while still warm – 10 minutes after they emerge from the oven. Chunks are like chips of chocolate, only bigger.

1. Mix the flour with the baking powder and salt.
2. Beat the butter, sugars, vanilla and egg until fluffy.
3. Blend in the flour, then the chocolate chunks and nuts. Chill this mixture for at least 1 hour to prevent overspreading during baking.
4. Drop the mixture in heaped tablespoonfuls on to an ungreased baking sheet, about 2 in (5 cm) apart.
5. Bake at 350°F (180°C) Gas 4 for 12–15 minutes or until lightly browned.
6. Cool for 2 minutes. Lift from the baking sheet on to wire racks to cool.

Makes 20 cookies

5 oz (150 g) plain flour
½ teaspoon baking powder
½ teaspoon salt
2½ oz (65 g) soft unsalted
   butter
2½ oz (65 g) granulated sugar
1 oz (25 g) brown sugar
1 teaspoon vanilla essence
1 medium egg
8 oz (225 g) chocolate, cut into
   chunks
3 oz (75 g) shelled walnuts,
   chopped

9

BREAKFASTS

A 'proper breakfast' as generally perceived is actually a sizeable meal which you happen to eat in the morning. Frequently it is a huge fry-up loaded with cholesterol so I suspect those who partake daily are on course for heart trouble.

The majority of us do not have time on a working day to eat grapefruit followed by cereal, followed by kippers or sausage, bacon and egg, followed by toast and marmalade, never mind prepare and cook all this stuff. But on a day off or holiday, especially if you intend to skip lunch, an English breakfast is a treat, worthy of some effort.

Breakfast customs vary. Continental breakfast is hotel-speak for no breakfast at all, just coffee and croissants as in France. There are more countries on the Continent than France, however, and in Holland, Germany and Switzerland you will usually find cold ham, salami and mild cheese on offer as well as muesli and boiled eggs. Americans go for sweet pastry, blueberry muffins and Danish pastries. All very delicious, but morning is a little early for sticky buns.

The stalwarts of the Edwardian breakfast, like kedgeree and kidneys, are much more interesting fare. As these are no longer commonly made, even in hotels, you may be quite pleasantly surprised at how appropriate something like home-made fish cakes are to this meal.

I don't agree with Somerset Maugham's famous quip about eating breakfast three times a day in order to dine well in England. I do find breakfast a waste, though, if served too soon after waking, and mourn the passing of early-morning – maybe not so early – tea followed at a decent interval by cooked breakfast. Those of us who find they become more fascinating, intelligent and alert late at night with the addition of a glass or two of red wine, can be daunted by cooked food too early in the morning. About an hour after rising, whenever that is, would be perfect.

Finally, the ideal breakfast is one cooked by somebody else. If you have, in your family, one of those people who just cannot sleep past 6 o'clock, this too could be perfect.

CORNED BEEF HASH WITH POACHED EGG

The key to successful corned beef hash is in the boiling of the potatoes. So few people in kitchens can successfully boil potatoes that I think it is worth including in the advanced practical examinations one day.

Firstly, if you are using peeled potatoes then use them shortly after they have been peeled and not when they have been sitting in a bucket of water for hours. Cut the potatoes into pieces of roughly equal thickness. If you are using unpeeled potatoes – which will give you a superior flavour and which is what I do myself – then carefully wash and sort the potatoes so that they are more or less the same size. You will need to peel them after cooking of course.

Next, use your head when choosing a saucepan. If you use one that is too big you will need to put in gallons of water in order to cover the potatoes. This will take ages to boil. Pour on water until the potatoes are just covered and then add plenty of salt and a tight-fitting lid. Bring the potatoes to the boil, and then turn the heat down so that they are boiling very gently. When they are completely cooked – after about 20 minutes – drain off the water. Replace the lid and let it stand for a minute while any excess water evaporates as steam. Don't leave the potatoes much longer than this or they will form a hard, dry layer that doesn't mash well.

Skin the potatoes if necessary. Add about ½ teaspoon salt and several turns of the pepper mill. Mash the potatoes. Do not put in any butter or liquid until the potatoes are completely mashed. If you are just making mashed potato you could add butter, milk or olive oil at this stage and start beating it. For corned beef hash you have no such worries.

The hash

Makes 10 patties

1 × 11¾ oz (340 g) tin corned beef
unsalted butter
1 large onion, peeled and roughly chopped
2 lb (900 g) white potatoes, cooked and mashed as above
black pepper
groundnut oil
1 fresh egg per person

1.   Open the tin. Try to avoid ripping off pieces of finger or swearing when the key breaks off half-way round the tin.
2.   Melt 1½ oz (40 g) of the butter in a large frying pan and then fry the onion until brown.
3.   Cut the corned beef into ½ in (1 cm) cubes and then add them to the pan. Empty the mixture into a bowl.
4.   Add the hot mashed potato, another 1½ oz (40 g) butter, and plenty of freshly ground black pepper.
5.   When the mixture has cooled you can form it into ten patties, roughly hamburger-shaped.
6.   Fry these as needed in a little groundnut oil combined with some butter. Always make sure the pan is hot and that the oil is hot before you put the corned beef hash in. This way you will get a golden crust and the hash will not stick too badly to the pan.

The eggs

7.   Bring a small saucepan of salted water to the boil. Crack a fresh egg into a saucer and then gently slide it into the water. Just 2 minutes later your poached egg should be perfect and can be lifted out with a slotted spoon, dried, and then placed on top of the corned beef hash.

I never use vinegar when poaching eggs as I have never discovered what good it was meant to do.

This is a simple recipe for a simple dish. It surprises me what a popular breakfast it makes. It surprises me even more how few people take the trouble to make simple things really well.

FISH CAKES

Whilst my head frequently feels delicate at breakfast time my palate does not. It is definitely the moment for kipper or bacon – or a fish cake. This recipe calls for smoked haddock. Crabmeat or salmon would be just as good. White fish, like cod, makes a more delicately flavoured fish cake if that suits you better.

Makes 4 portions

8 oz (225 g) smoked haddock
12 oz (350 g) potatoes
salt and freshly ground black
    pepper
1 oz (25 g) unsalted butter
1 teaspoon anchovy essence
2 medium eggs
1 sprig fresh parsley
4 oz (100 g) breadcrumbs, made
    from day-old white bread in
    a processor
groundnut oil for frying

1.   Poach the haddock in a minimum of water for about 3–4 minutes. Drain, and separate the fish into flakes.
2.   Peel the potatoes, cut them into even-sized pieces, boil in salted water, then drain and mash (see page 112).
3.   Season the mashed potato with salt and pepper. While it is still hot beat in the butter, anchovy essence and flaked fish.
4.   Break the eggs into a bowl, then lift one yolk out and beat this into the potato too.

It may be obvious to you but do bring the bowl containing the eggs right next to the pan with the fish and potato mixture, otherwise you will have slippery patches on the floor where the odd drip of egg white falls.
5.   Spread the mixture out to a thickness of ½ in (1 cm) on a plate and cool.
6.   Cut the cooled mixture into whatever shapes you prefer. Mix together the remaining egg whites and yolk. Chop the parsley and mix with the crumbs. Dip the fish cakes into the egg and then coat with breadcrumbs.
7.   Fry the fish cakes. Use enough oil to reach half-way up the fish cakes so that, when you have turned them over and they are crisp and brown both sides, there will be no edges uncooked.
8.   Serve with crisp bacon.

IRISH POTATO BREAD

These potato cakes are from Ulster where they are often served as part of a breakfast fry-up with bacon and egg. They also stand up to the grander company of foie gras terrine rather well, their earthy potato flavour giving a foil to foie gras' richness, which brioche does not.

1.   Peel the potatoes. Cut them into approximately equal-sized pieces, boil them in salted water until tender, then drain and mash (see page 112). Salt the potato well and stir in the butter. Allow to cool.
2.   Turn the mashed potato out on to a floured work surface. You need to incorporate about a third of its volume of plain flour. As you work in the flour the dough becomes easier to handle.
3.   Roll out the dough to ⅓ in (8 mm) thickness. Dust with a little flour and cut into whatever shapes take your fancy. Simple triangles leave no waste and suit me.
4.   Griddle the potato bread on a dry frying pan over moderate to low heat. Cook the pieces about 3 minutes on each side and then cool them on wire racks. Keep them in an airtight container in the fridge until needed, no longer than a couple of days.

Serves 4

1 lb (450 g) maincrop potatoes
salt
½ oz (15 g) unsalted butter
4 oz (100 g) plain flour

SALMON KEDGEREE

Almost as famous a breakfast dish as bacon and egg, but rather less widely cooked. The ratio of fish to rice is a question of taste and pocket. Most important is to fry the curry powder for a few seconds before adding the milky cream in which the fish has cooked. Forget this detail and the kedgeree will have a raw crude flavour.

1.   Place the salmon in an ovenproof dish, and season with salt and pepper. Pour in the milk and cream and the cover the dish with either a tight-fitting lid or silver foil. Bake in a moderate oven at 350°F (180°C) Gas 4 for 20 minutes until cooked.
2.   At the same time boil the rice in plenty of salted water, about 20 minutes. Drain off and keep to one side.
3.   In a medium-sized saucepan fry the chopped ginger in the butter until brown. Lift the pan off the heat and add the curry powder. Stir for a few seconds while the powder cooks.
4.   Pour on the cooking liquor from the salmon and bring to the boil. Let this simmer for 2 minutes.
5.   Add the rice. Shell the boiled eggs, roughly chop them and mix these also in the kedgeree.

Serves 4

8 oz (225 g) salmon fillet
salt and freshly ground black
   pepper
2½ fl oz (65 ml) milk
2½ fl oz (65 ml) double cream
4 oz (100 g) Patna rice
1 small knob ginger, chopped
1 oz (25 g) unsalted butter
1 teaspoon curry powder
2 hard-boiled eggs
juice of ½ lemon
a sprig of fresh parsley,
   chopped

6. Separate the fish into flakes and add to the saucepan.
7. Finish the kedgeree with a little lemon juice and roughly chopped parsley.

DEVILLED KIDNEYS

Serves 4

8 lamb's kidneys
salt
2 eggs
1 tablespoon prepared English mustard
1 teaspoon Worcestershire sauce
8 drops Tabasco
8 oz (225 g) fresh breadcrumbs
2 fl oz (50 ml) groundnut oil
2 oz (50 g) unsalted butter

These have fallen out of favour as a breakfast dish. I can see why. It's not a dish for the faint hearted in the morning. Best served with a strong, spicy Bloody Mary; if you are to have devilled kidneys for breakfast there is no point in being coy over vodka.

1. Skin the kidneys and cut them in quarters. Cut away any gristle. Sprinkle with a good pinch of salt.
2. Whisk together the eggs, mustard, Worcestershire sauce and Tabasco.
3. Coat the kidneys with this eggwash and then roll them in breadcrumbs.
4. Heat the oil in a large pan. Add the butter and when it is sizzling hot, fry the kidney for about 5 minutes until just done.
5. Lift the kidneys with a slotted spoon on to some kitchen paper to drain. Serve.

NATURAL YOGHURT WITH SOFT FRUIT, TOASTED NUTS AND HONEY

Serves 4

1 oz (25 g) flaked almonds
1 oz (25 g) hazelnuts
2 oz (50 g) toasted oat flakes
2 × 8 oz (225 g) tubs Greek-style natural yoghurt
2 tablespoons honey
2 bananas
1 × 8 oz (225 g) punnet ripe strawberries

Not so much a recipe as a compilation of fresh and easy things for a warm summer's morning. I used to sprinkle a product called Kretchmer's wheatgerm over the yoghurt but have recently had trouble obtaining it so now I use a mixture of toasted nuts and one of the many crunchy oat-based cereals.

There is no point in using low-fat yoghurt unless you actually prefer it. If you are worried about your weight, eat less or leave out the honey.

1. Toast the nuts and mix them with the oat flakes.
2. Divide the two tubs of yoghurt between four soup plates.
3. Put ½ tablespoonful of honey into the centre of each.
4. Slice the bananas and strawberries and arrange them on top.
5. Sprinkle with the crunchy nut mixture.

MARMALADE

Seville oranges come on to the market in early January so if you intend making marmalade this is the time, as the oranges don't keep well and are bulky to freeze.

Aim for a chunky marmalade, quite deep in colour. Small quantities like this aren't too much work and home-made marmalade is superior to anything you can buy. At Gidleigh Park we make 20 cases of Seville oranges into marmalade each January and towards the end it drives me nuts. This 3 lb (1.3 kg) batch shouldn't burden your sanity and will keep you in marmalade for a fair while.

Jams are generally simpler to make but, in truth, you can usually buy jam cheaper than make it, and the product will not be noticeably different.

Makes about 10 lb (4.5 kg)

3 lb (1.3 kg) Seville oranges
3 lemons
12 lb (5.4 kg) granulated or
  preserving sugar

1.   Wash the fruit. The skins of Seville oranges aren't treated with fungicides in the same way as dessert oranges so they are very prone to mould. Check your fruit is not affected as it taints the finished product. Remove any stalks.

2.   Boil the whole fruit in 6 pints (3.5 litres) water until soft, around 40 minutes.

3.   Strain the liquor obtained into a clean pot. Halve the fruit and scoop out the pith and pips into a sieve lined with clean cloth, preferably muslin. The juice from this is an important setting agent for the marmalade so squeeze out as much as possible before discarding the debris and add the juice to the pot.

4.   Slice the skins into strips.

5.   Add these strips to the pot and stir in the sugar. It is important to keep stirring until all the sugar is dissolved otherwise it cooks unevenly and is liable to crystallise later.

6.   Bring to the boil, then boil rapidly until setting point, probably 1½ hours. You test for setting point by lifting a tablespoonful from the pan on to a cold saucer. If it forms a skin it is ready.

7.   Sterilise the jars you intend to fill. The products sold for sterilising babies' bottles are ideal. Heat the jars and then fill them. Cover with little rounds of greaseproof paper, then cool. Screw down the tops of the jars (if using Kilner jars). Otherwise cover with cellophane.

10

STOCKS AND SAUCES

Stocks are the basis of many dishes, even in the apparently modern style of cooking, and it is essential that they are made carefully and properly. There is a widespread illusion in kitchens that stock must simmer for days and days to extract fully every ounce of flavour from the bones and vegetables. This is nonsense: if you cut the bones smaller they will obviously yield their flavour faster. In fact, what ruins many stocks is the mass of soggy vegetables endlessly overcooking in their hidden depths. Taste a leek or asparagus when it has boiled for ten minutes, then taste it again after six hours. It has not released its flavour – it has changed completely, becoming flabby, greasy and lifeless, and it has now shared this experience with the stock. When the vegetables have done their work take them out and throw them away; do the same with the bones and the meat. If your stock needs more power then reduce it once it is in liquid form.

Professional chefs are also very fond of the all-purpose stock. The stock is a separate ingredient with its own uses and its own merits. If you are making a wild mushroom soup or sauce you may sauté a few mushrooms with shallots and garlic and add that to the stock. A leek and potato soup will require a stock that is more complex, as the dish needs a deep base of flavour but not something intrusive. Carrots will sweeten the stock, aubergines will give body, caramelised onions will give a denser, more robust broth. Conversely, leeks can replace onions for more delicacy. Fresh herbs should be added towards the end of making a stock, and again provided they are really complementary. These must not be overcooked as they may turn bitter and damage the stock.

Sauces

Consider what you want from a sauce. Certainly dry food needs something to moisten it, a sauce or a creamy vegetable. I have divided the subject into its two main strands, stock sauces and relishes, each having a different purpose and characteristics.

Professional cooks adore sauce-making and the sauce cook's position is always one of the kitchen's most exalted. Perhaps because it is the final job on each plate, an opportunity for fine tuning and should draw all the ingredients on that plate together into a cohesive dish.

Stock sauces, where possible, should derive from whatever meat, fish or vegetable you are cooking; pan juices mixed with stock or broth made from all the trimmings, carcass, debris, cooked out with aromatic vegetables and water. There is a feeling of both satisfaction and rectitude in using up everything, extracting all the flavour without any waste.

Steer clear of bouillon cubes, certainly in sauces. A chicken gizzard has an incomparably better, more intense, flavour to release than any commercial cube, yet most go straight into the dustbin. Tap water is always preferable. It may dilute the sauce's strength but it will at least not add anything salty, chemical or nasty to it.

Stock for sauces made from roast bones has a more developed flavour in the same way that roast meat has in relation to boiled meat. Your objective is a clear, clean taste; fish stock that tastes unmistakably of fish, chicken likewise, never an aftertaste of cheap white wine. Strong herbs are a bad idea for the same reason, you want veal stock and sauce that tastes of veal, not tarragon or thyme. You may build into the finished sauce any complexities of flavour. For these building blocks, bases to keep and freeze, your aim is a simplicity of flavour.

Relish sauces do not grow out of a dish in the same way as stock-based sauces. Rather they add some new and extra dimension, providing contrast or balance, enlivening ingredients in the way a salad dressing does for lettuce, horseradish cream for smoked trout or Béarnaise sauce for grilled meat or fish.

I have included two sweet sauces, but not fruit coulis. Delicious though it is, I'm not sure it is a sauce any more than runny mashed potato is. It is a combination of fruit and sugar, heated and liquidised. How much sugar you will need depends entirely on how sweet or ripe the fruit is. A recipe confuses the issue.

CHICKEN CONSOMME

This can be a versatile soup, garnished with some pasta threads and a poached scallop for a soup course. Its main purpose in my kitchen, though, is as an ingredient, and so I make it without salt.

The stock

Makes 2 pints (1.2 litres)

Stock
2 lb (900 g) chicken winglets or carcasses
8 oz (225 g) onions, peeled
8 oz (225 g) leeks, washed
1 garlic clove, peeled
1 teaspoon groundnut oil
1 teaspoon black peppercorns

Clarification
2 egg whites
1 tablespoon tomato purée
8 oz (225 g) mixed peeled and chopped leeks, carrots and onions
1 chicken leg, boned and cut into small pieces

1. Roast the winglets or carcasses in a moderately hot oven – 400°F (200°C) Gas 6 – until golden brown, about 20 minutes.
2. Roughly chop the vegetables and then pan-fry in the oil until lightly coloured.
3. Lift the winglets and vegetables into a large saucepan. Discard any grease or residual oil from the pans and deglaze them by boiling 1 pint (600 ml) water in first the frying pan then the roasting tray. Pour this liquor on to the bones.
4. Add a further 3 pints (1.65 litres) water and the peppercorns, bring to the boil and skim. Let the stock simmer for 1 hour, and skim periodically, topping up with fresh water as necessary, so that you end up with 4 pints (2.25 litres) of stock.

The clarification

5. Combine the clarification ingredients in a food processor. The clarification mixture works better if it is well chilled. Many cooks mix ice cubes into it at this stage.
6. Skim any fat from the 4 pints (2.25 litres) stock and add the stock to the other ingredients in a large pot.
7. Bring to the boil. You should stir the stock regularly as it comes to the boil, as it has a tendency to stick to the pot base and burn. When the stock arrives at boiling point all the clarifying ingredients will form a white crust, underneath which you should have a crystal clear consommé.
8. Allow the consommé to simmer very gently for 1 hour, then strain it through wet muslin.
9. Reduce the consommé by gentle boiling until you have 2 pints (1.2 litres).

VEAL SAUCE BASE

If you have the time, pots and inclination this dark sauce base is invaluable. Like stock it freezes well. Mixed with roasting juices of duck or beef it makes a good vehicle for quite complex flavours. It is made in two stages, preferably on separate days. Initially you make a good stock from bones. The next day you convert this stock into a more full-bodied sauce base. Don't put any salt in either stock or sauce base.

Stage 1

1. Roast the bones in a hot oven – 450°F (230°C) Gas 8 – until brown, probably 30 minutes.
2. Pan-fry the vegetables in groundnut oil until coloured.
3. Lift the bones and vegetables into a clean pot. Discard any fat from the roasting tray. Pour in a pint (600 ml) cold water and bring it to the boil to deglaze. Pour this and a further 3 pints (1.65 litres) of water over the bones and vegetables and bring to the boil.
4. Reduce the heat so that the stock simmers and cooks slowly for 4 hours. Skim off any impurities that rise to the surface as scum, and top up the stock with water periodically so that you still end up with 4 pints (2.25 litres) of liquid.
5. Decant the stock into a container and discard the bones and vegetables which remain. Allow this to cool. When cold, refrigerate until you are ready to embark on Stage 2. Any fat or grease which is in the stock will rise to the surface during this time and solidify. Lift this away.

Stage 2

6. Bring the stock back to the boil.
7. Pan-fry the beef, onion and garlic separately, then add the tomato purée.
8. Pour the wine on to the beef and let it boil almost to nothing. Add the contents of the pan to the stock, along with the sugar and pepper.
9. Simmer for 2 hours. Let it reduce by half, adding a little cold water from time to time to bring impurities to the surface for you to skim off.
10. Strain the sauce base through fine muslin, discarding the beef and vegetables, and allow to set. Use as required.

Makes 2 pints (900 ml)

Stage 1

2 lb (900 g) veal bones, cut into 2 in (5 cm) pieces
8 oz (225 g) coarsely cut mixture of onion, leeks and carrot
1 tablespoon groundnut oil

Stage 2

8 oz (225 g) shin of beef, diced
1 onion, peeled
1 garlic clove, peeled
1 tablespoon tomato purée
2 fl oz (50 ml) red wine
1 teaspoon sugar
freshly ground black pepper

FISH STOCK

Fish stock will become cloudy and bitter if boiled too long with the bones. To concentrate the flavour you should boil down the stock after it has been decanted from the bones. It freezes very well in ice-cube trays.

Makes 1 pint (600 ml)

2 lb (900 g) white fish bones
1 oz (25 g) unsalted butter
1 onion, peeled and sliced
1 leek, peeled and sliced
2 fl oz (50 ml) dry white wine
1 sprig fresh parsley
1 teaspoon black peppercorns

1. Run cold water over the fish bones for 5 minutes to wash them.
2. Choose a large saucepan and melt the butter in it. Sweat the vegetables for 3–4 minutes without colouring, then add the fish bones.
3. Stir the bones, so that they don't stick, until they are sealed by the heat, then add the white wine, parsley, peppercorns and 2 pints (900 ml) water.
4. Bring to the boil. Reduce heat and simmer for 20 minutes.
5. Strain the stock into a clean pot and then re-boil. Reduce by simmering until halved in volume. Keep for no more than 2 days in the fridge.

TARRAGON SAUCE

Makes 1 pint (600 ml)

1 pint (600 ml) chicken
    consommé (see page 119)
½ teaspoon arrowroot
2 fl oz (50 ml) double cream
2 sprigs fresh tarragon,
    chopped
1 sprig fresh parsley, chopped
1 small bunch chives, snipped
lemon juice
salt and freshly ground black
    pepper

This sauce needs quite a concentrated chicken flavour to compete with the sharp herbs, hence the reduction of the chicken consommé. A little arrowroot will help hold the sauce together, and save any further reduction.

Use it with breast of chicken, roast chicken or any other white meat.

1. Reduce the chicken consommé by half by gentle boiling.
2. Moisten the arrowroot with a little water and slightly thicken the consommé with it.
3. Add the cream and stir in well.
4. Add the chopped and snipped herbs to the sauce.
5. Bring the sauce back to the boil, once only, and adjust the balance with a little lemon juice and salt and pepper to taste.

MEAUX MUSTARD AND CAPER SAUCE

Serves 4

4 tablespoons Meaux mustard
3 fl oz (75 ml) red wine
5 fl oz (150 ml) veal sauce base
    (see opposite)
5 fl oz (150 ml) double cream
1 oz (25 g) unsalted butter
1 oz (25 g) capers
salt and freshly ground black
    pepper

This sauce is creamy and rich, made with the veal sauce base opposite. I serve it with grilled beef or veal.

1. Whisk the mustard and red wine together.
2. Bring to the boil, then add the veal sauce base.
3. Add cream then boil hard for 2 minutes before whisking in the butter.
4. Finish the sauce with capers, salt and pepper. If you are not fond of capers you may substitute a teaspoonful of lemon juice.

VERMOUTH AND RED PEPPER SAUCE

Especially good with meaty, white fish like turbot. This recipe yields just over a pint (600 ml).

1. Gently stew the pieces of red pepper, shallots and garlic in olive oil for 5 minutes without browning.
2. Add the stock. Bring to the boil and then simmer for 20 minutes.
3. Add the vermouth and then liquidise in a blender.
4. Return the liquidised sauce to the pan and re-boil it. Add the cream.
5. Whisk in the butter, lemon juice, salt and pepper.
6. Pass through muslin, and reheat gently as and when needed.

Makes 1 pint (600 ml)

2 red peppers, de-seeded and cut into 1 in (2.5 cm) pieces
2 shallots, peeled and chopped
1 small garlic clove, peeled and chopped
1 tablespoon olive oil
1 pint (600 ml) fish stock (see previous page)
2 fl oz (50 ml) dry vermouth
1 fl oz (25 ml) double cream
2 oz (50 g) unsalted butter
juice of ½ lemon
salt and freshly ground black pepper

WHITE BUTTER SAUCE

For steamed fish or vegetables. This sauce will taste greasy if poured on anything fried or roasted. The variations and permutations are endless. Try adding ginger and chives to accompany scallops or steamed salmon; try basil and chopped tomato with Dover sole.

All white butter sauces need either lemon juice or a vinegar reduction to taste as they should – sharp and fresh, never greasy or fat.

Salted butter is especially useless for this sauce. It is very salty when warm, has too much residual sediment and is in any case too sweet.

1. Sweat the shallots without colouring in a knob of the butter for 3 or 4 minutes.
2. Add the vinegar and white wine. Boil rapidly until the liquid has reduced by half.
3. Take the pan off the heat and whisk in 1 oz (25 g) only of the butter. When the butter is completely incorporated add one more ounce (25 g) of butter and whisk it in.
4. Whisk in the remaining butter ounce by ounce. Periodically return the pan to the heat and bring the sauce up to near boiling point.
5. When all the butter is incorporated you should have a smooth velvety sauce. Pour in the lemon juice. Season with salt and cayenne pepper, then strain through muslin.

Serves 4

4 shallots, peeled and finely chopped
8 oz (225 g) unsalted butter
1 tablespoon white wine vinegar
5 fl oz (150 ml) dry white wine
juice of 1 lemon
salt
a pinch of cayenne pepper

MAYONNAISE

Makes 10 fl oz (300 ml)

4 egg yolks
salt and freshly ground black
    pepper
1 tablespoon white wine
    vinegar
5 fl oz (150 ml) olive oil
5 fl oz (150 ml) sunflower seed
    oil

Very small quantities of mayonnaise are impossible. This makes 10 fl oz (300 ml). Any left over will keep for days in a refrigerator. You may substitute lemon juice for vinegar if you wish or add a teaspoonful of French mustard at the start.

1.   Put the egg yolks in a bowl and season with salt and pepper.
2.   Whisk in the vinegar.
3.   If the oils are cold then warm them slightly. Whisk them into the egg yolks drop by drop at first. Then, as the mayonnaise thickens, you can whisk them in a little more quickly.

SALAD CREAM

No connection with anything commercially bottled. This type of dressing will make a refreshing change from mayonnaise or other oil-based dressings.

Serves 4

2 hard-boiled eggs
salt and freshly ground white
    pepper
a pinch of cayenne pepper
¼ teaspoon caster sugar
5 fl oz (150 ml) double cream
juice of ½ lemon

1.   Separate the hard-boiled eggs into yolk and white. Chop the white and keep to garnish the finished sauce.
2.   Make a paste of the yolks with the seasonings, a teaspoonful of water and the sugar.
3.   Incorporate the cream slowly by trickling it into the egg yolks, stirring constantly.
4.   Add lemon juice. Pour into a sauce boat and decorate with the chopped egg whites.

MUSTARD DRESSING

Serves 4

1 tablespoon Dijon mustard
1 small egg yolk
1 tablespoon white wine
    vinegar
salt and freshly ground black
    pepper
2 tablespoons olive oil
2 tablespoons groundnut oil

This is my standard salad dressing. If you have a particularly good, intense olive oil, don't use it here. Use all groundnut oil and then just a few drops of olive oil straight on to the leaves. You can make a larger quantity if you wish and keep in an empty oil bottle. It keeps for a week without any problem.

1.   Put the Dijon mustard in a small bowl or cup.
2.   Add the egg yolk and stir in with a spoon.
3.   Stir in the vinegar until completely combined. Add salt and pepper.
4.   Slowly trickle in the oils, stirring constantly. You should have an emulsified dressing which will deliver the same ratio of oil, mustard and vinegar to each lettuce leaf.

HORSERADISH SAUCE

This sauce is at a strength suitable for smoked fish, cold meats, fish pâtés. For roast beef use half the quantity of cream.

1.   Peel the horseradish and grate it. Horseradish is at its most powerful around the outside of the root so grate across it for an even consistency.
2.   Stir in the mustard, sugar and lemon juice.
3.   Whisk the cream separately and fold it into the horseradish. Finish with a pinch of salt.

Serves 4

2 oz (50 g) horseradish
1 tablespoon French mustard
1 tablespoon caster sugar
juice of ½ lemon
6 fl oz (175 ml) double cream
salt

CUSTARD

There are comparatively few important sweet sauces. This and fruit coulis are the most common and the most versatile. Custard is a good base for many flavours. Try almond, cocoa or orange and Cointreau. It can be churned as ice cream either straight as vanilla or with any ingredient that takes your fancy.

This recipe looks simple but needs great care especially when adding boiling milk to the egg yolk and sugar mixture, and again when cooking out the sauce. Too much cooking or carelessness will give a grainy sauce. Too little cooking produces a medium which is paradise for bacteria and a stomach problem around the corner.

1.   Whisk the sugar and egg yolks together until the colour pales to white and the texture becomes creamy.
2.   Chop the vanilla pod. Drop it into the milk and bring the milk to the boil.
3.   Trickle the milk on to the egg yolk and sugar mixture, whisking continually.
4.   Return the pan to a very low heat and stir the custard over it for 5 minutes by which time it should have slightly but perceptibly thickened. The custard is cooked.
5.   Strain the sauce through muslin into a clean container. If not for immediate use, refrigerate as soon as the custard cools.

Serves 4

4 oz (100 g) caster sugar
8 egg yolks
1 vanilla pod
1 pint (600 ml) milk

SABAYON

This sauce is served either hot or cold. To use warm just complete the first stage of the recipe. For a cold sauce or indeed a delightful chilled dessert, carry on with the second stage.

Stage 1

Serves 4

Stage 1
6 egg yolks
4 oz (100 g) caster sugar
a pinch of salt
4 fl oz (120 ml) sweet white wine

Stage 2
4 fl oz (120 ml) double cream

1. Heat a pot of water that is big enough to hold your whisking bowl without Archimedes' principle causing a flood on the stove. When the water is simmering, put all the ingredients except the cream into the bowl, preferably stainless steel, and then place the bowl in the water.
2. Whisk the ingredients together vigorously for 10 minutes, by which time they will have risen in volume and be thick and creamy.

Stage 2

3. Transfer the bowl on to another container, this time filled with a mixture of ice cubes and water. Whisk the sabayon vigorously until it is quite cold.
4. Whip the cream and fold it into the sabayon.

INDEX

ACKNOWLEDGMENTS

I should like to thank Kay and Paul Henderson of Gidleigh Park who encouraged me to write this book, and advised me throughout. I would also like to express thanks to Helen Robinson, who typed the manuscript and was unfailingly polite about its contents.